most loved recipe collection

most
loved
treats

Pictured on Front Cover:
Candy Bar Squares, page 92

Pictured on Back Cover:
Banana Macadamia Sundaes, page 66

Most Loved Treats
Copyright © Company's Coming Publishing Limited

Second Printing February 2005

National Library of Canada Cataloguing in Publication
Paré, Jean
    Most loved treats / Jean Paré.

(Most loved recipe collection)
Includes index.
ISBN 1-896891-90-X

    1. Desserts. I. Title. II. Series: Paré, Jean. Most loved recipe collection.

TX773.P35911 2004   641.8'6   C2004-901697-0

Published by
Company's Coming Publishing Limited
2311 – 96 Street
Edmonton, Alberta, Canada T6N 1G3
Tel: 780-450-6223   Fax: 780-450-1857
www.companyscoming.com

Company's Coming is a registered trademark owned by Company's Coming Publishing Limited

Printed in China

We gratefully acknowledge the following suppliers for their generous support of our Test Kitchen and Photo Studio:

Corelle®
Hamilton Beach® Canada
Lagostina®
Proctor Silex® Canada
Tupperware®

Our special thanks to the following businesses for providing extensive props for photography:

Anchor Hocking Canada
Canhome Global
Casa Bugatti
Cherison Enterprises Inc.
Danesco Inc.
Island Pottery Inc.
Klass Works
Linens 'N Things
Michaels The Arts And Crafts Store
Mikasa Home Store
Pfaltzgraff Canada
Pier 1 Imports
Stokes
The Royal Doulton Store
Zellers

Pictured from left: Chocolate Orange Cake, page 6; Swedish Tea Cakes, page 34; Nanaimo Squares, page 72; Mars Bars Squares, page 74; Bocconne Dolce, page 52.

table of contents

the Company's Coming story

"never share a recipe you wouldn't use yourself"

Jean Paré grew up understanding that the combination of family, friends and home cooking is the essence of a good life. From her mother she learned to appreciate good cooking, while her father praised even her earliest attempts. When she left home she took with her many acquired family recipes, a love of cooking and an intriguing desire to read recipe books like novels!

In 1963, when her four children had all reached school age, Jean volunteered to cater the 50th anniversary of the Vermilion School of Agriculture, now Lakeland College. Working out of her home, Jean prepared a dinner for over 1000 people which launched a flourishing catering operation that continued for over eighteen years. During that time she was provided with countless opportunities to test new ideas with immediate feedback—resulting in empty plates and contented customers! Whether preparing cocktail sandwiches for a house party or serving a hot meal for 1500 people, Jean Paré earned a reputation for good food, courteous service and reasonable prices.

"Why don't you write a cookbook?" Time and again, as requests for her recipes mounted, Jean was asked that question. Jean's response was to team up with her son, Grant Lovig, in the fall of 1980 to form Company's Coming Publishing Limited. April 14, 1981 marked the debut of "150 DELICIOUS SQUARES," the first Company's Coming cookbook in what soon would become Canada's most popular cookbook series.

Jean Paré's operation has grown steadily from the early days of working out of a spare bedroom in her home. Full-time staff includes marketing personnel located in major cities across Canada. Home Office is based in Edmonton, Alberta in a modern building constructed specially for the company.

Today the company distributes throughout Canada and the United States in addition to numerous overseas markets, all under the guidance of Jean's daughter, Gail Lovig. Best-sellers many times over in English, Company's Coming cookbooks have also been published in French and Spanish. Familiar and trusted in home kitchens around the world, Company's Coming cookbooks are offered in a variety of formats, including the original softcover series.

Jean Paré's approach to cooking has always called for quick and easy recipes using everyday ingredients. Even when travelling, she is constantly on the lookout for new ideas to share with her readers. At home, she can usually be found researching and writing recipes, or working in the company's test kitchen. Jean continues to gain new supporters by adhering to what she calls "the golden rule of cooking:" never share a recipe you wouldn't use yourself. It's an approach that works—*millions of times over!*

foreword

Most Loved Treats is the third volume in our Most Loved Recipe Collection and is especially compiled to satisfy your sweet tooth. Whether you crave something quick and delicious to top off your supper or something slow and sweet to linger over with coffee or tea, you're sure to find the perfect treat among these time-honoured favourites. Every recipe is easy to follow and uses common ingredients you most likely have on hand, but results in extraordinary treats you didn't know you could make at home. Try it! You'll find you can almost taste that first bite with your eyes!

Dessert is the grand finale at mealtime. I usually follow a heavier meal with a light dessert, but I go all out with dessert if the meal is lighter. To help you choose just the right treat for the occasion, we've organized the recipes in this book into five convenient sections. You'll find every recipe photographed in scrumptious colour. When you have some extra time to spend in the kitchen, select something from the Cakes & Cheesecakes section to show off your culinary skills. When you have the urge to bake something soft, chocolate or nutty for snacking, Cookies has just what you need. Looking for a more substantial treat? Try any one of our delightful Desserts. The section on Squares, Bars & Brownies is stacked full of bite-size bliss, and Sweet Snacks is filled with those oh-so-tempting favourites you just can't do without.

Want something extra special to complete the tasty treat you've just made? Why not display it to full advantage on a brightly coloured serving plate or on delicate china? Add fruit garnishes or chocolate curls and you're all set for company! And remember, the next treat you make could become your newest family tradition—because the best part of making something sweet is sharing it with those you love.

With this superb collection of *Most Loved Treats*, you'll never be at a loss when company's coming, even if it's only a company of one—you!

Jean Paré

nutrition information

Each recipe has been analyzed using the most up-to-date version of the Canadian Nutrient File from Health Canada, which is based on the United States Department of Agriculture (USDA) Nutrient Data Base. If more than one ingredient is listed (such as "hard margarine or butter"), or a range is given (1 – 2 tsp., 5 – 10 mL) then the first ingredient or amount is used in the analysis. Where an ingredient reads "sprinkle," "optional," or "for garnish," it is not included as part of the nutrition information. Milk, unless stated otherwise, is 1% and cooking oil, unless stated otherwise, is canola.

Margaret Ng, B.Sc. (Hon), M.A.
Registered Dietitian

Milk chocolate flavour with a splash of orange. A delicious dessert to serve any time.

Chocolate Orange Cake

Hard margarine (or butter), softened	1/2 cup	125 mL
Granulated sugar	3/4 cup	175 mL
Large eggs	2	2
Orange flavouring	2 tsp.	10 mL
Semi-sweet chocolate baking squares (1 oz., 28 g, each), chopped	3	3
Sour milk (see Note)	3/4 cup	175 mL
All-purpose flour	2 cups	500 mL
Baking soda	1 tsp.	5 mL
Salt	1/2 tsp.	2 mL
CHOCOLATE ORANGE ICING		
Icing (confectioner's) sugar	4 cups	1 L
Block of cream cheese, softened	8 oz.	250 g
Cocoa, sifted if lumpy	1/2 cup	125 mL
Hard margarine (or butter), softened	1/4 cup	60 mL
Orange flavouring	2 tsp.	10 mL

Cream margarine and sugar in large bowl. Add eggs, 1 at a time, beating well after each addition. Add orange flavouring. Beat well.

Heat and stir chocolate and sour milk in heavy medium saucepan on medium-low until chocolate is melted. Mixture will look curdled. Remove from heat. Let stand for 5 minutes.

Combine flour, baking soda and salt in medium bowl. Add to margarine mixture in 3 additions, alternating with chocolate mixture in 2 additions, beginning and ending with flour mixture. Divide and spread evenly in 2 greased 8 inch (20 cm) round pans. Bake in 350°F (175°C) oven for about 25 minutes until wooden pick inserted in centre comes out clean. Let stand in pans for 5 minutes before inverting onto wire racks to cool completely.

Chocolate Orange Icing: Beat all 5 ingredients in medium bowl until smooth. Makes about 3 cups (750 mL) icing. Place 1 cake layer on serving plate. Spread with 3/4 cup (175 mL) icing. Place second layer on top. Spread top and side with remaining icing. Cuts into 12 wedges.

1 wedge: 538 Calories; 23.3 g Total Fat (11.2 g Mono, 1.8 g Poly, 9 g Sat); 59 mg Cholesterol; 80 g Carbohydrate; 2 g Fibre; 7 g Protein; 430 mg Sodium

Pictured on page 7.

A recipe this old and this good lasts through the years and stands the test of time. You can omit the topping and use as a shortcake.

Lazy Daisy Cake

Large eggs	2	2
Granulated sugar	1 cup	250 mL
Vanilla	1 tsp.	5 mL
All-purpose flour	1 cup	250 mL
Baking powder	1 tsp.	5 mL
Salt	1/2 tsp.	2 mL
Milk	1/2 cup	125 mL
Hard margarine (or butter)	1 tbsp.	15 mL
COCONUT TOPPING		
Hard margarine (or butter)	3 tbsp.	50 mL
Brown sugar, packed	1/2 cup	125 mL
Half-and-half cream (or milk)	2 tbsp.	30 mL
Flake coconut	1/2 cup	125 mL

Beat eggs in medium bowl until frothy. Add sugar, 2 tbsp. (30 mL) at a time while beating, until thickened. Add vanilla. Beat well.

Combine flour, baking powder and salt in small bowl. Add to egg mixture. Stir.

Heat and stir milk and margarine in small heavy saucepan on medium until margarine is melted. Add to flour mixture. Stir well. Spread batter evenly in greased 9 x 9 inch (22 x 22 cm) pan. Bake in 350°F (175°C) oven for 25 to 30 minutes until wooden pick inserted in centre comes out clean.

Coconut Topping: Measure margarine, brown sugar and cream into medium saucepan. Bring to a rolling boil on medium-high, stirring occasionally. Remove from heat.

Add coconut. Stir. Spread evenly over warm cake. Return to oven for about 3 minutes until top is bubbling. Let stand in pan on wire rack until cool. Cuts into 12 pieces.

1 piece: 226 Calories; 7.7 g Total Fat (3.1 g Mono, 0.6 g Poly, 3.6 g Sat); 37 mg Cholesterol; 37 g Carbohydrate; 1 g Fibre; 3 g Protein; 198 mg Sodium

Pictured on page 9.

Very pretty, moist cake with a tangy lime bite. Serve with Juicy Berries for an extra-special treat.

juicy berries

Combine 2 cups (500 mL) whole fresh berries (such as blackberries, blueberries or raspberries) and sliced strawberries in medium bowl. Add 1 cup (250 mL) white grape juice and 1/2 cup (125 mL) white corn syrup. Stir gently until coated. Chill for 1 hour to blend flavours. Serve with Lime Poppy Seed Cake.

juicy berries variation

Ice wine is a slightly more expensive, but delightful way to flavour berries. Omit white grape juice and corn syrup. Add 1/2 to 3/4 cup (125 to 175 mL) ice wine to 1 1/2 to 3 cups (375 to 750 mL) berries. Stir gently. A sweet dessert wine may be used instead of ice wine.

Lime Poppy Seed Cake

Milk	1 cup	250 mL
Poppy seeds	3 tbsp.	50 mL
Egg whites (large), room temperature	3	3
Almond flavouring	1 tsp.	5 mL
Hard margarine (or butter), softened	1 cup	250 mL
Granulated sugar	1 1/4 cups	300 mL
Egg yolks (large)	3	3
Finely grated lime zest	1 tbsp.	15 mL
All-purpose flour	2 cups	500 mL
Baking powder	1 tbsp.	15 mL
Salt	1/2 tsp.	2 mL
Hot water	2 tbsp.	30 mL
Icing (confectioner's) sugar	3/4 cup	175 mL
Lime juice	6 tbsp.	100 mL

Heat and stir milk and poppy seeds in small saucepan on medium until very hot, but not boiling. Remove from heat. Let stand until room temperature.

Beat egg whites and flavouring in medium bowl until stiff peaks form. Set aside.

Cream margarine and granulated sugar in large bowl. Add egg yolks, lime zest and milk mixture. Beat well.

Combine flour, baking powder and salt in small bowl. Add to margarine mixture. Beat well. Fold egg white mixture into flour mixture until no white streaks remain. Spread evenly in greased 10 inch (25 cm) angel food tube pan or 10 inch (25 cm) springform pan. Bake in 325°F (160°C) oven for about 1 hour until wooden pick inserted in centre of cake comes out clean. Let stand in pan for 10 minutes before removing to serving plate.

Stir hot water into icing sugar in small bowl until smooth. Add lime juice. Stir. Drizzle over hot cake, allowing syrup to soak in. Cool. Cuts into 12 wedges.

1 wedge: 384 Calories; 18.8 g Total Fat (11.2 g Mono, 2.6 g Poly, 4 g Sat); 55 mg Cholesterol; 50 g Carbohydrate; 1 g Fibre; 5 g Protein; 408 mg Sodium

Pictured on page 11.

Rich and delicious. Very moist. Freezes well.

Date Cake

Chopped pitted dates	1 1/2 cups	375 mL
Baking soda	1 1/2 tsp.	7 mL
Boiling water	1 1/2 cups	375 mL
Hard margarine (or butter), softened	3/4 cup	175 mL
Brown sugar, packed	1 cup	250 mL
Granulated sugar	1/2 cup	125 mL
Large eggs	2	2
Vanilla	1 tsp.	5 mL
All-purpose flour	2 1/2 cups	625 mL
Baking powder	1 1/2 tsp.	7 mL
Salt	1/2 tsp.	2 mL
Hard margarine (or butter)	1/3 cup	75 mL
Brown sugar, packed	1 cup	250 mL
Half-and-half cream (or milk)	3 tbsp.	50 mL
Fine coconut	1 cup	250 mL

Place dates in medium bowl. Sprinkle with baking soda. Pour boiling water over top. Set aside until cool. Stir.

Cream next 3 ingredients in large bowl. Add eggs, 1 at a time, beating well after each addition. Add vanilla. Beat.

Combine flour, baking powder and salt in small bowl. Add to margarine mixture in 3 additions, alternating with date mixture in 2 additions, beginning and ending with flour mixture. Spread evenly in greased 9 x 13 inch (22 x 33 cm) pan. Bake in 325°F (160°C) oven for 40 to 50 minutes until wooden pick inserted in centre comes out clean.

Measure next 3 ingredients into medium saucepan. Bring to a rolling boil on medium-high, stirring occasionally. Remove from heat.

Add coconut. Stir. Spread evenly over warm cake. Return to oven for about 3 minutes until top is bubbling. Let stand in pan on wire rack until cool. Cuts into 18 pieces.

1 piece: 365 Calories; 15.4 g Total Fat (7.7 g Mono, 1.3 g Poly, 5.5 g Sat); 24 mg Cholesterol; 56 g Carbohydrate; 2 g Fibre; 3 g Protein; 347 mg Sodium

Pictured on page 13.

A warm and comforting dessert on a chilly winter evening.

Sticky Ginger Fig Cake

Chopped figs	1 1/3 cups	325 mL
Baking soda	1 tsp.	5 mL
Boiling water	1 1/3 cups	325 mL
Hard margarine (or butter), softened	1/3 cup	75 mL
Brown sugar, packed	2/3 cup	150 mL
Large eggs	2	2
All-purpose flour	1 cup	250 mL
Baking powder	2 tsp.	10 mL
Minced crystallized ginger	1/4 cup	60 mL
CINNAMON BRANDY SAUCE		
Hard margarine (or butter), cut up	1/2 cup	125 mL
Brown sugar, packed	1/2 cup	125 mL
Whipping cream	1/2 cup	125 mL
Brandy	2 tbsp.	30 mL
Ground cinnamon	1/2 tsp.	2 mL

Place figs in medium bowl. Sprinkle with baking soda. Pour boiling water over top. Let stand for 10 minutes. Process (with liquid) in blender or food processor until almost smooth.

Cream margarine and brown sugar in large bowl. Add eggs, 1 at a time, beating well after each addition.

Combine flour, baking powder and ginger in small bowl. Add to margarine mixture. Stir well. Add fig mixture. Stir. Line bottom and side of greased 8 inch (20 cm) springform pan with parchment (not waxed) paper. Spread batter evenly in pan. Bake in 350°F (175°C) oven for about 50 minutes until wooden pick inserted in centre of cake comes out clean. Let stand in pan for 10 minutes before removing to wire rack to cool.

Cinnamon Brandy Sauce: Heat and stir all 5 ingredients in medium saucepan on medium until boiling. Boil for about 5 minutes, without stirring, until slightly thickened. Let stand for 5 minutes. Makes 1 cup (250 mL) sauce. Drizzle over individual servings of warm cake. Cuts into 8 wedges.

1 wedge: 545 Calories; 27 g Total Fat (15.2 g Mono, 2.6 g Poly, 7.8 g Sat); 72 mg Cholesterol; 73 g Carbohydrate; 4 g Fibre; 5 g Protein; 530 mg Sodium

Pictured on page 15.

Simple and delicious. Dust with icing sugar instead of the icing for a less sweet dessert.

White Chocolate Pound Cake

White chocolate baking squares (1 oz., 28 g, each), chopped	4	4
Evaporated milk	1 cup	250 mL
Hard margarine (or butter), softened	1 cup	250 mL
Granulated sugar	1 2/3 cups	400 mL
Large eggs	5	5
All-purpose flour	2 3/4 cups	675 mL
Baking soda	1/2 tsp.	2 mL
Salt	1/2 tsp.	2 mL
WHITE CHOCOLATE ICING		
Hard margarine (or butter)	1/4 cup	60 mL
White chocolate baking squares (1 oz., 28 g, each), chopped	3	3
Icing (confectioner's) sugar	2 cups	500 mL
Milk	1 tbsp.	15 mL
Vanilla	1/2 tsp.	2 mL

Heat and stir chocolate and evaporated milk in heavy medium saucepan on medium-low until chocolate is melted. Remove from heat. Let stand for 5 minutes.

Cream margarine and sugar in large bowl. Add eggs, 1 at a time, beating well after each addition.

Combine flour, baking soda and salt in medium bowl. Add to margarine mixture in 3 additions, alternating with chocolate mixture in 2 additions, beginning and ending with flour mixture. Spread evenly in greased 12 cup (3 L) bundt pan. Bake in 325°F (160°C) oven for about 1 hour until wooden pick inserted in centre of cake comes out clean. Let stand in pan for 20 minutes before inverting onto wire rack to cool completely.

White Chocolate Icing: Heat margarine and chocolate in small heavy saucepan on lowest heat, stirring often, until chocolate is almost melted. Do not overheat. Remove from heat. Stir until smooth.

Add icing sugar, milk and vanilla. Beat until smooth. Add more milk if necessary until barely pourable consistency. Drizzle over cake. Cuts into 16 wedges.

1 wedge: 467 Calories; 20.7 g Total Fat (11.7 g Mono, 1.9 g Poly, 5.8 g Sat); 71 mg Cholesterol; 65 g Carbohydrate; 1 g Fibre; 7 g Protein; 343 mg Sodium

Pictured on page 17.

A pretty contrast—amber pumpkin on dark gingersnap crust. Tastes as good as it looks. Make a day ahead. Freezes well.

Pumpkin Cheesecake

GINGERSNAP CRUMB CRUST

Hard margarine (or butter)	1/4 cup	60 mL
Finely crushed gingersnap cookies	1 1/4 cups	300 mL

FILLING

Blocks of cream cheese (8 oz., 250 g, each), softened	2	2
Granulated sugar	2/3 cup	150 mL
Large eggs	2	2
Can of pure pumpkin (no spices)	14 oz.	398 mL
Ground cinnamon	1/2 tsp.	2 mL
Ground nutmeg	1/2 tsp.	2 mL
Ground ginger	1/2 tsp.	2 mL
Salt	1/2 tsp.	2 mL

Gingersnap Crumb Crust: Melt margarine in medium saucepan. Remove from heat. Add crushed gingersnaps. Stir well. Press firmly in ungreased 9 inch (22 cm) springform pan. Bake in 350°F (175°C) oven for 10 minutes. Let stand until cool.

Filling: Beat cream cheese and sugar in large bowl until smooth. Add eggs, 1 at a time, beating after each addition until just combined.

Add remaining 5 ingredients. Beat well. Spread evenly over crust. Bake for 50 to 60 minutes until centre is almost set. Run knife around inside edge of pan to allow cheesecake to settle evenly. Let stand in pan on wire rack until cooled completely. Chill overnight. Cuts into 12 wedges.

1 wedge: 302 Calories; 20.7 g Total Fat (7.8 g Mono, 1.2 g Poly, 10.5 g Sat); 82 mg Cholesterol; 25 g Carbohydrate; 1 g Fibre; 5 g Protein; 360 mg Sodium

Pictured on page 19.

Garnish with whipped topping and whole cookies for an extra-special look that's sure to make the kids smile.

Cookie Cheesecake

COOKIE CRUMB CRUST

Hard margarine (or butter)	2 tbsp.	30 mL
Finely crushed cream-filled chocolate cookies	1 1/2 cups	375 mL

FILLING

Blocks of light cream cheese (8 oz., 250 g, each), softened	3	3
Granulated sugar	1 cup	250 mL
Vanilla	1 1/2 tsp.	7 mL
Whipping cream	1 cup	250 mL
Large eggs	3	3
Coarsely chopped cream-filled chocolate cookies	1 cup	250 mL

Cookie Crumb Crust: Melt margarine in medium saucepan. Remove from heat. Add crushed cookies. Stir well. Press firmly in bottom and 1/2 inch (12 mm) up side of greased 10 inch (25 cm) springform pan.

Filling: Beat cream cheese, sugar and vanilla in large bowl until smooth. Add whipping cream. Beat. Add eggs, 1 at a time, beating after each addition until just combined.

Fold in chopped cookies until evenly distributed. Spread evenly over crust. Bake in 325°F (160°C) oven for about 1 1/4 hours until centre is almost set. Run knife around inside edge of pan to allow cheesecake to settle evenly. Let stand in pan on wire rack until cooled completely. Chill overnight. Cuts into 16 wedges.

1 wedge: 318 Calories; 20.2 g Total Fat (7.7 g Mono, 1.2 g Poly, 9.7 g Sat); 88 mg Cholesterol; 28 g Carbohydrate; trace Fibre; 7 g Protein; 452 mg Sodium

Pictured on page 21.

Mint and chocolate make a refreshing after-dinner dessert. Made using a microwave oven. Serve with a hot cup of coffee or a cool glass of milk.

Crème de Menthe Cheesecake

CHOCOLATE CRUMB CRUST

Hard margarine (or butter)	1/4 cup	60 mL
Chocolate wafer crumbs	1 1/4 cups	300 mL
Granulated sugar (optional)	2 tbsp.	30 mL

FILLING

Blocks of cream cheese (4 oz., 125 g, each), softened	3	3
Granulated sugar	1/2 cup	125 mL
Large eggs	2	2
Mint-flavoured liqueur (such as green Crème de Menthe)	1/3 cup	75 mL

CHOCOLATE SOUR CREAM TOPPING

Semi-sweet chocolate chips	1/2 cup	125 mL
Sour cream	1/2 cup	125 mL

Chocolate Crumb Crust: Place margarine in microwave-safe medium bowl. Microwave, uncovered, on high (100%) for about 35 seconds until melted. Add wafer crumbs and sugar. Stir well. Press firmly in bottom and up side of 9 inch (22 cm) microwave-safe pie plate. Microwave, uncovered, on high (100%) for 2 minutes. Set aside.

Filling: Beat cream cheese and sugar in large bowl until smooth. Add eggs, 1 at a time, beating after each addition until just combined. Add liqueur. Beat well. Spread evenly in crust. Cover with waxed paper. Microwave on medium (50%) for about 10 minutes, turning dish halfway through baking time if microwave doesn't have turntable, until centre is set. Let stand for 5 minutes.

Chocolate Sour Cream Topping: Place chips in 1 cup (250 mL) liquid measure. Microwave, uncovered, on medium (50%) for about 2 minutes until almost melted. Do not overheat. Stir until smooth. Add sour cream. Stir well. Spread evenly over filling. Chill for 3 to 4 hours until set. Cuts into 8 wedges.

1 wedge: 486 Calories; 31.6 g Total Fat (12.1 g Mono, 1.9 g Poly, 15.8 g Sat); 111 mg Cholesterol; 41 g Carbohydrate; 1 g Fibre; 7 g Protein; 340 mg Sodium

Pictured on page 23.

An attractive, rosy-coloured dessert. Cream cheese and cherries are always a favourite.

Cherry Chilled Cheesecake

GRAHAM CRUMB CRUST

Hard margarine (or butter)	1/3 cup	75 mL
Graham cracker crumbs	1 1/4 cups	300 mL
Brown sugar, packed	2 tbsp.	30 mL

FILLING

Block of cream cheese, softened	8 oz.	250 g
Icing (confectioner's) sugar	1 1/2 cups	375 mL
Vanilla	1/2 tsp.	2 mL
Can of cherry pie filling	19 oz.	540 mL
Frozen whipped topping, thawed (or whipped cream)	2 cups	500 mL

Graham Crumb Crust: Melt margarine in medium saucepan. Remove from heat. Add graham crumbs and brown sugar. Stir well. Reserve 3 tbsp. (50 mL) crumb mixture in small cup. Press remaining mixture firmly in ungreased 9 x 9 inch (22 x 22 cm) pan. Bake in 350°F (175°C) oven for 10 minutes. Let stand in pan on wire rack until cooled completely.

Filling: Beat cream cheese, icing sugar and vanilla in medium bowl until smooth. Add pie filling. Stir well. Spread evenly over crust.

Spread whipped topping evenly over filling. Sprinkle reserved crumb mixture over top. Chill overnight. Cuts into 12 pieces.

1 piece: 329 Calories; 17 g Total Fat (6.2 g Mono, 1 g Poly, 8.8 g Sat); 23 mg Cholesterol; 43 g Carbohydrate; 1 g Fibre; 3 g Protein; 189 mg Sodium

Pictured on page 27.

Mini-Chip Cheesecakes

This make-ahead dessert is a favourite with young and old. Garnish with whipped topping and chocolate curls.

Chocolate wafers	12	12
Blocks of light cream cheese (8 oz., 250 g, each), softened	2	2
Granulated sugar	3/4 cup	175 mL
Large eggs	2	2
Vanilla	1 tsp.	5 mL
Mini semi-sweet chocolate chips	1/2 cup	125 mL
Mini semi-sweet chocolate chips	1/2 cup	125 mL

Line 12 ungreased muffin cups with large paper liners. Place 1 wafer in bottom of each liner.

Beat cream cheese and sugar in medium bowl until smooth. Add eggs, 1 at a time, beating after each addition until just combined. Add vanilla. Beat.

Heat first amount of chips in small heavy saucepan on lowest heat, stirring often, until chocolate is almost melted. Do not overheat. Remove from heat. Stir until smooth. Add to cream cheese mixture. Stir.

Fold second amount of chips into cream cheese mixture until evenly distributed. Divide and spoon over wafers. Bake in 325°F (160°C) oven for 25 to 30 minutes until set. Let stand in pan on wire rack until cool. Chill for 2 to 3 hours. Makes 12 mini-cheesecakes.

1 mini-cheesecake: 255 Calories; 14.2 g Total Fat (4.8 g Mono, 0.6 g Poly, 7.8 g Sat); 62 mg Cholesterol; 29 g Carbohydrate; 1 g Fibre; 6 g Protein; 338 mg Sodium

Pictured on page 27.

This treat has a built-in topping—no icing required.

Cheesy Cupcakes

Block of light cream cheese, softened	8 oz.	250 g
Granulated sugar	1/2 cup	125 mL
Large egg	1	1
Semi-sweet chocolate chips	1 cup	250 mL
All-purpose flour	1 1/2 cups	375 mL
Granulated sugar	1 cup	250 mL
Cocoa, sifted if lumpy	1/3 cup	75 mL
Baking soda	1 tsp.	5 mL
Salt	1/2 tsp.	2 mL
Hard margarine (or butter), softened	6 tbsp.	100 mL
Warm water	1 cup	250 mL
Vanilla	1 tsp.	5 mL

Beat cream cheese, first amount of sugar and egg in small bowl until smooth. Add chips. Stir. Set aside.

Combine next 5 ingredients in large bowl. Make a well in centre.

Add margarine, warm water and vanilla to well. Beat for about 2 minutes until smooth. Line 20 ungreased muffin cups with large paper liners. Divide and spoon batter into each cup. Divide and spoon cream cheese mixture over batter. Bake in 350°F (175°C) oven for 30 to 35 minutes until wooden pick inserted in centre of cupcake comes out clean. Makes 20 cupcakes.

1 cupcake: 207 Calories; 9.1 g Total Fat (4.1 g Mono, 0.6 g Poly, 3.9 g Sat); 19 mg Cholesterol; 30 g Carbohydrate; 1 g Fibre; 3 g Protein; 256 mg Sodium

Pictured on page 27.

Top Right: Cheesy Cupcakes, above
Centre Left: Mini-Chip Cheesecakes, page 25
Bottom Right: Cherry Chilled Cheesecake, page 24

A wonderful blend of flavours in a sweet, chewy macaroon! Almost too pretty to eat—but not quite!

Cherry Coconut Macaroons

Flake coconut	2 cups	500 mL
Maraschino cherries, blotted dry and chopped	3/4 cup	175 mL
Sliced almonds, toasted (see Note)	1/2 cup	125 mL
All-purpose flour	1/2 cup	125 mL
Salt	1/4 tsp.	1 mL
Egg whites (large)	4	4
Almond flavouring	1/2 tsp.	2 mL
Granulated sugar	1/2 cup	125 mL

Combine first 5 ingredients in medium bowl.

Beat egg whites and flavouring on medium in large bowl until frothy. Add sugar, 1 tbsp. (15 mL) at a time while beating, until soft peaks form. Fold coconut mixture into egg white mixture until just moistened. Drop, using 2 tbsp. (30 mL) for each, about 2 inches (5 cm) apart, onto greased cookie sheets. Bake in 325°F (160°C) oven for about 15 minutes until edges are golden. Let stand on cookie sheets for 5 minutes before removing to wire racks to cool. Makes about 2 1/2 dozen (30) macaroons.

1 macaroon: 85 Calories; 5.1 g Total Fat (0.8 g Mono, 0.3 g Poly, 3.7 g Sat); 0 mg Cholesterol; 9 g Carbohydrate; 1 g Fibre; 2 g Protein; 30 mg Sodium

Pictured on page 29.

Top Right: Cherry Coconut Macaroons, above
Centre Left: Cranberry Chip Cookies, page 30
Bottom: Pecan Caramel Kisses, page 31

Festive, flavourful cookies that will satisfy any sweet craving!

Cranberry Chip Cookies

Large eggs	2	2
Brown sugar, packed	1 2/3 cups	400 mL
Vanilla	1 tsp.	5 mL
All-purpose flour	1 3/4 cups	425 mL
Baking powder	1 tsp.	5 mL
Baking soda	1/2 tsp.	2 mL
Cooking oil	1/2 cup	125 mL
Dried cranberries	1/2 cup	125 mL
Unsalted peanuts	1/2 cup	125 mL
White chocolate chips	1/2 cup	125 mL

Beat eggs, brown sugar and vanilla in large bowl until light and creamy.

Combine flour, baking powder and soda in small bowl. Add to egg mixture. Stir well.

Add remaining 4 ingredients. Stir until evenly distributed. Cover. Chill for 1 hour. Roll dough into balls, using 1 tbsp. (15 mL) for each. Arrange balls, about 2 inches (5 cm) apart, on greased cookie sheets. Bake in 350°F (175°C) oven for about 15 minutes until golden. Let stand on cookie sheets for 5 minutes before removing to wire racks to cool. Makes about 3 1/2 dozen (42) cookies.

1 cookie: 107 Calories; 4.6 g Total Fat (2.4 g Mono, 1.2 g Poly, 0.8 g Sat); 11 mg Cholesterol; 16 g Carbohydrate; 1 g Fibre; 1 g Protein; 33 mg Sodium

Pictured on page 29.

Pecan Caramel Kisses

Egg whites (large), room temperature	2	2
Cream of tartar	1/8 tsp.	0.5 mL
Maple flavouring	1/4 tsp.	1 mL
Icing (confectioner's) sugar	1 cup	250 mL
Chopped pecans, toasted (see Note)	1/3 cup	75 mL
Caramels	10	10
Milk	2 tsp.	10 mL

Beat egg whites, cream of tartar and flavouring in medium bowl until stiff peaks form. Add icing sugar, 2 tbsp. (30 mL) at a time while beating, until very glossy and stiff.

Fold pecans into egg white mixture until evenly distributed. Drop, using 1 tbsp. (15 mL) for each, about 2 inches (5 cm) apart, onto greased parchment (not waxed) paper-lined cookie sheets. Bake in 275°F (140°C) oven for about 30 minutes until dry and edges are golden. Let stand on cookie sheets for 5 minutes before removing to wire racks to cool.

Heat and stir caramels and milk in small saucepan on medium-low until smooth. Remove from heat. Let stand for 5 minutes. Drizzle over meringues. Makes about 2 1/2 dozen (30) meringues.

1 meringue: 37 Calories; 1.2 g Total Fat (0.6 g Mono, 0.2 g Poly, 0.3 g Sat); 0 mg Cholesterol; 7 g Carbohydrate; trace Fibre; 0 g Protein; 10 mg Sodium

Pictured on page 29.

Light and crispy meringues drizzled with sticky caramel sauce. Crunchy toasted pecans make this an immensely satisfying sweet treat.

note

To toast nuts, place in single layer in ungreased shallow pan. Bake in 350°F (175°C) oven for 5 to 8 minutes, stirring or shaking often, until desired doneness.

These often don't make it from the cookie sheet to the cookie jar! A little expensive to make, but simply irresistible.

variation

For smaller cookies, roll dough into 1 1/2 inch (3.8 cm) balls. Arrange balls, about 2 inches (5 cm) apart, on greased cookie sheets. Flatten cookies slightly with flat-bottomed glass dipped in second amount of granulated sugar. Bake in 375°F (190°C) oven for 8 to 10 minutes until golden. Let stand on cookie sheets for 5 minutes before removing to wire racks to cool. Makes about 5 dozen (60) cookies.

Giant Candy Bar Cookies

Hard margarine (or butter), softened	1 cup	250 mL
Granulated sugar	1 cup	250 mL
Brown sugar, packed	1 cup	250 mL
Large eggs	2	2
Vanilla	2 tsp.	10 mL
All-purpose flour	2 cups	500 mL
Baking powder	1 tsp.	5 mL
Baking soda	1 tsp.	5 mL
Salt	1/2 tsp.	2 mL
Quick-cooking rolled oats (not instant)	2 1/3 cups	575 mL
Chocolate-covered crispy toffee bars (such as Skor or Heath), 1 1/2 oz. (39 g) each, chopped	8	8
Granulated sugar	1/4 cup	60 mL

Cream margarine, first amount of granulated sugar and brown sugar in large bowl. Add eggs, 1 at a time, beating well after each addition. Add vanilla. Beat.

Combine next 4 ingredients in small bowl. Add to margarine mixture. Stir until just moistened.

Add rolled oats and chocolate bar pieces. Stir well. Roll into 2 inch (5 cm) balls. Arrange 4 to 6 balls, about 4 inches (10 cm) apart, on greased cookie sheet.

Dip flat-bottomed glass into second amount of granulated sugar. Flatten cookies to 1/2 inch (12 mm) thickness, dipping glass in sugar as necessary. Bake in 375°F (190°C) oven for about 11 minutes until golden. Let stand on cookie sheet for 5 minutes before removing to wire rack to cool. Repeat with remaining dough. Makes about 3 dozen (36) cookies.

1 cookie: 204 Calories; 9.2 g Total Fat (3.8 g Mono, 0.8 g Poly, 1.3 g Sat); 17 mg Cholesterol; 29 g Carbohydrate; 1 g Fibre; 3 g Protein; 168 mg Sodium

Pictured on page 33.

Also known as Swedish Pastry and Thumbprints. So good, you'll need to make more!

Swedish Tea Cakes

Hard margarine (or butter), softened	1/2 cup	125 mL
Brown sugar, packed	1/4 cup	60 mL
Egg yolk (large)	1	1
All-purpose flour	1 cup	250 mL
Baking powder	1/2 tsp.	2 mL
Salt	1/8 tsp.	0.5 mL
Egg white (large), fork-beaten	1	1
Finely chopped nuts (your favourite), for coating	2/3 cup	150 mL
Jam or jelly (red is best), your favourite	6 tbsp.	100 mL

Cream margarine and brown sugar in large bowl. Add egg yolk. Beat well.

Combine flour, baking powder and salt in small bowl. Add to margarine mixture. Stir until stiff dough forms. Roll dough into balls, using 2 tsp. (10 mL) for each.

Dip balls into egg white. Roll in nuts. Arrange balls, about 2 inches (5 cm) apart, on greased cookie sheets. Dent each with thumb. Bake in 325°F (160°C) oven for 5 minutes. Remove from oven. Press dents again. Bake for 10 to 15 minutes until golden. Let stand on cookie sheets for 5 minutes before removing to wire racks.

Fill each dent with 1 tsp. (5 mL) jam. (Unfilled tea cakes may be stored in airtight container and filled with jam just before serving.) Makes about 20 tea cakes.

1 tea cake: 125 Calories; 7.7 g Total Fat (3.8 g Mono, 2.2 g Poly, 1.2 g Sat); 11 mg Cholesterol; 13 g Carbohydrate; 1 g Fibre; 2 g Protein; 88 mg Sodium

Pictured on page 35.

These are definitely more impressive than regular cookies but still easy enough for kids to make! A tasty one-bite snack that will make you popular with kids and grown-ups alike.

cookie pizza

Press 3 cups (750 mL) cookie dough evenly in greased 12 inch (30 cm) pizza pan. Sprinkle with semi-sweet chocolate chips, butterscotch chips, candy-coated chocolate candies (such as Smarties or M & M's), cereal flakes, coconut, peanuts or any other favourites. Bake in 375°F (190°C) oven for 12 to 15 minutes until puffy and golden. Serve warm or cold. Cuts into 16 wedges.

Peanut Butter Hide-Aways

Hard margarine (or butter), softened	1/2 cup	125 mL
Smooth peanut butter	1/2 cup	125 mL
Granulated sugar	1/3 cup	75 mL
Brown sugar, packed	1/3 cup	75 mL
Large egg	1	1
All-purpose flour	1 1/3 cups	325 mL
Baking powder	1 tsp.	5 mL
Baking soda	1/2 tsp.	2 mL
Salt	1/4 tsp.	1 mL
Miniature peanut butter cups	36	36

Beat first 4 ingredients in large bowl until light and creamy. Add egg. Beat well.

Combine next 4 ingredients in small bowl. Add to margarine mixture. Stir until just moistened. Dough will be stiff. Roll into 36 balls, using 1 tbsp. (15 mL) for each. Place 1 ball in each of 36 ungreased mini-muffin cups. Bake in 375°F (190°C) oven for about 10 minutes until puffy and golden. Remove from oven.

Remove and discard foil cup from peanut butter cups. Press 1 peanut butter cup into each hot cookie. Loosen edges of cookies with tip of knife. Chill for 20 minutes before removing from pan. If cookies are difficult to remove, tap bottom of pan several times on hard surface or let stand until cookies are room temperature. Makes 3 dozen (36) cookies.

1 cookie: 120 Calories; 7.3 g Total Fat (3.5 g Mono, 1.1 g Poly, 2.1 g Sat); 7 mg Cholesterol; 12 g Carbohydrate; 1 g Fibre; 3 g Protein; 119 mg Sodium

Pictured on page 39.

Oatmeal Chip Cookies

Hard margarine (or butter), softened	1 cup	250 mL
Brown sugar, packed	2 cups	500 mL
Large eggs	2	2
Vanilla	1 tsp.	5 mL
All-purpose flour	2 cups	500 mL
Baking powder	1 tsp.	5 mL
Baking soda	1/2 tsp.	2 mL
Quick-cooking rolled oats (not instant)	2 cups	500 mL
Semi-sweet chocolate chips	2 cups	500 mL
Medium unsweetened coconut	3/4 cup	175 mL

Beat margarine and sugar in large bowl until light and creamy. Add eggs, 1 at a time, beating well after each addition. Add vanilla. Beat.

Combine flour, baking powder and soda in small bowl. Add to margarine mixture. Stir well.

Add remaining 3 ingredients. Stir until well distributed. Drop, using 2 tbsp. (30 mL) for each, about 2 inches (5 cm) apart, onto greased cookie sheets. Bake in 350ºF (175ºC) oven for 8 to 10 minutes until golden. Let stand on cookie sheets for 5 minutes before removing to wire racks to cool. Makes about 5 dozen (60) cookies.

1 cookie: 126 Calories; 6.2 g Total Fat (2.9 g Mono, 0.5 g Poly, 2.5 g Sat); 7 mg Cholesterol; 17 g Carbohydrate; 1 g Fibre; 2 g Protein; 61 mg Sodium

Pictured below.

Chocolate and oatmeal make the ultimate cookie. A great favourite.

oatmeal chip pizza

Press 3 cups (750 mL) cookie dough evenly in greased 12 inch (30 cm) pizza pan. Sprinkle with semi-sweet chocolate chips, butterscotch chips, candy-coated chocolate candies (such as Smarties or M & M's), cereal flakes, coconut, peanuts or any other favourites. Bake in 350ºF (175ºC) oven for 12 to 15 minutes until golden. Cuts into 16 wedges.

These delicious cookies contain no flour. Soft and chewy. Makes a huge batch. Use an extra-large bowl, plastic tub or roaster to mix these.

rainbow chip pizza

Press 3 cups (750 mL) cookie dough evenly in greased 12 inch (30 cm) pizza pan. Sprinkle with semi-sweet chocolate chips, butterscotch chips, candy-coated chocolate candies (such as Smarties or M & M's), cereal flakes, coconut, peanuts or any other favourites. Bake in 350°F (175°C) oven for 12 to 15 minutes until golden. Cuts into 16 wedges.

Rainbow Chip Cookies

Smooth peanut butter	6 cups	1.5 L
Brown sugar, packed	6 cups	1.5 L
Granulated sugar	4 cups	1 L
Hard margarine (or butter), softened	2 cups	500 mL
Large eggs	12	12
Vanilla	1 tbsp.	15 mL
Golden corn syrup	1 tbsp.	15 mL
Quick-cooking rolled oats (not instant)	18 cups	4.5 L
Semi-sweet chocolate chips	2 cups	500 mL
Candy-coated chocolate candies (such as Smarties or M & M's)	2 cups	500 mL
Baking soda	8 tsp.	40 mL

Beat first 4 ingredients in extra-large bowl until light and creamy. Add eggs, 2 at a time, beating well after each addition. Add vanilla and corn syrup. Beat.

Add remaining 4 ingredients. Stir well. Roll into balls, using 2 tbsp. (30 mL) for each. Arrange balls, about 2 inches (5 cm) apart, on greased cookie sheets. Flatten slightly. Bake in 350°F (175°C) oven for 7 to 8 minutes until golden. Overbaking will make them hard. Let stand on cookie sheets for 5 minutes before removing to wire racks to cool. Makes about 26 dozen (312) cookies.

1 cookie: 108 Calories; 5.2 g Total Fat (2.4 g Mono, 1 g Poly, 1.1 g Sat); 8 mg Cholesterol; 14 g Carbohydrate; 1 g Fibre; 3 g Protein; 78 mg Sodium

Pictured on page 39.

Top Left: Rainbow Chip Cookies, above
Bottom Right: Peanut Butter Hide-Aways, page 36

Pretty, 3-layered cookie. Freezes well before, or after, baking.

Icebox Ribbons

Hard margarine (or butter), softened	1 cup	250 mL
Granulated sugar	1 cup	250 mL
Large egg	1	1
Vanilla	1 tsp.	5 mL
All-purpose flour	2 1/2 cups	625 mL
Baking powder	1 tsp.	5 mL
Salt	1/4 tsp.	1 mL
Red liquid (or paste) food colouring		
Chopped red glazed cherries	1/4 cup	60 mL
Medium unsweetened coconut	1/3 cup	75 mL
Semi-sweet chocolate chips	1/3 cup	75 mL
Chopped nuts (your favourite)	1/3 cup	75 mL

Cream margarine and sugar in large bowl. Add egg and vanilla. Beat well.

Combine flour, baking powder and salt in medium bowl. Add to margarine mixture. Stir until stiff dough forms. Divide dough into 3 equal portions.

Knead enough red food colouring into 1 portion of dough until pink. Add cherries. Knead until evenly distributed. Press in foil-lined 8 x 4 x 3 inch (20 x 10 x 7.5 cm) loaf pan.

Add coconut to second portion of dough. Knead until evenly distributed. Press evenly over pink layer.

Heat chips in small heavy saucepan on lowest heat, stirring often, until almost melted. Do not overheat. Remove from heat. Stir until smooth. Add chocolate and nuts to third portion of dough. Knead until no streaks remain. Press evenly over coconut layer. Cover with plastic wrap. Chill overnight. Remove from pan. Remove and discard foil. Cut into 1/4 inch (6 mm) thick slices. Cut each slice into 3 pieces. Arrange slices, about 2 inches (5 cm) apart, on greased cookie sheets. Bake in 350°F (175°C) oven for 10 to 12 minutes until edges are golden. Let stand on cookie sheets for 5 minutes before removing to wire racks to cool. Makes about 5 1/2 dozen (66) cookies.

1 cookie: 72 Calories; 4 g Total Fat (2.1 g Mono, 0.6 g Poly, 1.1 g Sat); 3 mg Cholesterol; 8 g Carbohydrate; trace Fibre; 1 g Protein; 50 mg Sodium

Pictured on page 43.

Noodle Power

Semi-sweet chocolate chips	1 cup	250 mL
Butterscotch chips	1 cup	250 mL
Hard margarine (or butter)	1/4 cup	60 mL
Smooth peanut butter	1/4 cup	60 mL
Dry chow mein noodles	2 cups	500 mL
Unsalted peanuts	1 cup	250 mL

These little stacks are shiny and ever so good. They are softer to bite into than other similar cookies.

Heat first 4 ingredients in large heavy saucepan on lowest heat, stirring often, until chips are almost melted. Do not overheat. Remove from heat. Stir until smooth.

Add noodles and peanuts. Stir until coated. Mixture will be soft. Drop, using 2 tsp. (10 mL) for each, onto waxed paper-lined cookie sheets. Let stand until set. May be chilled to hasten setting. Makes 2 1/2 dozen (30) cookies.

1 cookie: 123 Calories; 8.3 g Total Fat (3.7 g Mono, 1.9 g Poly, 2.2 g Sat); 0 mg Cholesterol; 12 g Carbohydrate; 1 g Fibre; 2 g Protein; 47 mg Sodium

Pictured on page 42.

Coconut Peaks

Flake coconut	3 cups	750 mL
Icing (confectioner's) sugar	2 cups	500 mL
Hard margarine (or butter), melted	1/4 cup	60 mL
Half-and-half cream (or milk)	2 tbsp.	30 mL
Semi-sweet chocolate chips	1 cup	250 mL
Hard margarine (or butter)	1 tbsp.	15 mL

These will take the spotlight on any plate of cookies! A no-bake treat that freezes well.

Combine first 4 ingredients in large bowl. Roll into balls, using 1/2 tbsp. (7 mL) for each. Squeeze tops to form peaks that resemble haystacks. Arrange on waxed paper-lined cookie sheet. Chill, uncovered, overnight.

Heat chips and second amount of margarine in small heavy saucepan on lowest heat, stirring often, until chips are almost melted. Do not overheat. Remove from heat. Stir until smooth. Dip peaks of cookies into chocolate mixture. Let stand until chocolate is set. Makes 2 1/2 dozen (30) cookies.

1 cookie: 143 Calories; 10 g Total Fat (2.2 g Mono, 0.3 g Poly, 7 g Sat); 0 mg Cholesterol; 15 g Carbohydrate; 1 g Fibre; 1 g Protein; 28 mg Sodium

Pictured on page 42.

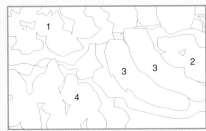

Photo Legend next page
1. Noodle Power, this page
2. Coconut Rum Diagonals, page 44
3. Icebox Ribbons, page 40
4. Coconut Peaks, this page

Pretty diamond-shaped cookies with an awesome flavour combination.

coconut diagonals

Omit the rum flavouring. Use same amount of vanilla.

Coconut Rum Diagonals

Hard margarine (or butter), softened	1/2 cup	125 mL
Granulated sugar	1/4 cup	60 mL
Vanilla	1 tsp.	5 mL
Salt	1/8 tsp.	0.5 mL
All-purpose flour	1 cup	250 mL
Flake coconut	1 cup	250 mL
Baking powder	1/2 tsp.	2 mL

RUM ICING

Icing (confectioner's) sugar	1 cup	250 mL
Water	1 1/2 tbsp.	25 mL
Rum flavouring	1/2 tsp.	2 mL

Beat first 4 ingredients in large bowl until light and creamy.

Combine flour, coconut and baking powder in small bowl. Add to margarine mixture. Stir well. Divide dough into 6 equal portions. Roll each portion into 9 inch (22 cm) rope. Arrange ropes, about 2 inches (5 cm) apart, on greased cookie sheets. Bake in 350°F (175°C) oven for 18 to 22 minutes until golden. Let stand on cookie sheets on wire racks for 5 minutes.

Rum Icing: Stir all 3 ingredients in small bowl, adding more water or icing sugar if necessary until spreading consistency. Ice ropes while still warm. Cut each rope into 1 inch (2.5 cm) diagonals, for a total of 4 1/2 dozen (54) cookies.

1 diagonal: 50 Calories; 3 g Total Fat (1.2 g Mono, 0.2 g Poly, 1.4 g Sat); 0 mg Cholesterol; 6 g Carbohydrate; trace Fibre; 0 g Protein; 31 mg Sodium

Pictured on page 43.

These melt in your mouth! Garnish with your favourite Christmas candy.

Whipped Shortbread

Butter (not margarine), softened	1 cup	250 mL
Granulated sugar	1/2 cup	125 mL
All-purpose flour	1 1/2 cups	375 mL
Cornstarch	1/4 cup	60 mL

Beat butter and sugar in medium bowl until light and creamy.

(continued on next page)

Combine flour and cornstarch in small bowl. Add to butter mixture, 2 tbsp. (30 mL) at a time while beating, until smooth. Pipe 1 1/2 inch (3.8 cm) rosettes, about 2 inches (5 cm) apart, onto ungreased cookie sheets. Bake in 375°F (190°C) oven for 12 to 14 minutes until just golden. Let stand on cookie sheets for 5 minutes before removing to wire racks to cool. Makes 2 1/2 dozen (30) cookies.

1 cookie: 99 Calories; 6.6 g Total Fat (1.9 g Mono, 0.3 g Poly, 4.1 g Sat); 18 mg Cholesterol; 10 g Carbohydrate; trace Fibre; 1 g Protein; 66 mg Sodium

Pictured on page 47.

Candy Cane Cookies

Hard margarine (or butter), softened	1 cup	250 mL
Icing (confectioner's) sugar	1 cup	250 mL
Large egg	1	1
Almond flavouring	1 tsp.	5 mL
Vanilla	1 tsp.	5 mL
Peppermint flavouring	1/4 tsp.	1 mL
All-purpose flour	2 1/2 cups	625 mL
Baking powder	1 tsp.	5 mL
Salt	1 tsp.	5 mL
Red liquid food colouring	1/2 tsp.	2 mL

A fun cookie for the whole family to make together.

Beat first 6 ingredients in large bowl until light and creamy.

Combine flour, baking powder and salt in medium bowl. Add to margarine mixture. Stir until stiff dough forms. Divide dough into 2 equal portions.

Knead food colouring into 1 portion of dough until evenly tinted. Roll about 1 tsp. (5 mL) of each colour dough into 5 1/2 inch (14 cm) rope. Lay side by side. Pinch ends together. Twist and form into candy cane shape. Repeat with remaining dough. Arrange, about 2 inches (5 cm) apart, on greased cookie sheets. Bake in 350°F (175°C) oven for about 10 minutes until just golden. Let stand on cookie sheets for 5 minutes before removing to wire racks to cool. Makes about 4 1/2 dozen (54) cookies.

1 cookie: 65 Calories; 3.7 g Total Fat (2.4 g Mono, 0.4 g Poly, 0.8 g Sat); 4 mg Cholesterol; 7 g Carbohydrate; trace Fibre; 1 g Protein; 94 mg Sodium

Pictured on page 47.

These freeze well—a great way to get a head start on your holiday baking.

variations

Sprinkle with granulated sugar or sanding (decorating) sugar (see Note) before baking.

Outline shape of baked cookies with Easy Glaze, this page.

note

Sanding sugar is a coarse decorating sugar that comes in white and various colours and is available at specialty kitchen stores.

to decorate baked cookies:

Add more water or icing sugar until barely pourable consistency. Paint glaze onto cookies with small paintbrush. Sprinkle with coloured sanding (decorating) sugar (see Note).

Spoon into piping bag fitted with small plain writing tip or small resealable freezer bag with tiny piece snipped off corner. Pipe small dots or outline edge on cookie. Add gold or silver dragées if desired.

Sugar Cookies

Hard margarine (or butter), softened	3/4 cup	175 mL
Granulated sugar	3/4 cup	175 mL
Large egg	1	1
Vanilla	1 tsp.	5 mL
All-purpose flour	2 cups	500 mL
Baking soda	1 tsp.	5 mL
Cream of tartar	1 tsp.	5 mL
Ground cardamom (optional)	1/4 tsp.	1 mL
Salt	1/4 tsp.	1 mL

Cream margarine and sugar in large bowl. Add egg and vanilla. Beat well.

Combine remaining 5 ingredients in medium bowl. Add to margarine mixture. Stir until stiff dough forms. Roll dough out to 1/8 inch (3 mm) thickness on lightly floured surface. Cut out dough using lightly floured cookie cutters. Arrange cookies, about 2 inches (5 cm) apart, on greased cookie sheets. Bake in 350°F (175°C) oven for about 10 minutes until golden. Let stand on cookie sheets for 5 minutes before removing to wire racks to cool. Makes 7 dozen (84) cookies.

1 cookie: 35 Calories; 1.8 g Total Fat (1.2 g Mono, 0.2 g Poly, 0.4 g Sat); 3 mg Cholesterol; 4 g Carbohydrate; trace Fibre; 0 g Protein; 43 mg Sodium

Pictured on page 47.

Easy Glaze

Water	2 tsp.	10 mL
Icing (confectioner's) sugar	1/2 cup	125 mL
Liquid (or paste) food colouring		

Stir water into icing sugar in small bowl, adding more water or icing sugar if necessary until spreading consistency. Add food colouring, 1 drop at a time, stirring well after each addition until desired colour is reached. Makes about 6 tbsp. (100 mL).

1 batch of icing: 247 Calories; 0.1 g Total Fat (0 g Mono, 0 g Poly, 0 g Sat); 0 mg Cholesterol; 63 g Carbohydrate; 0 g Fibre; 0 g Protein; 1 mg Sodium

Pictured on page 47 (on Sugar Cookies).

Top Left: Candy Cane Cookies, page 45
Top Right: Whipped Shortbread, page 44
Bottom Left: Sugar Cookies, this page

Tell the kids they can have cookies for breakfast—they'll love it!

Nutri-Cookies

Hard margarine (or butter), softened	1/2 cup	125 mL
Smooth peanut butter	1/2 cup	125 mL
Liquid honey	1 cup	250 mL
Large eggs	2	2
Vanilla	1 tsp.	5 mL
Quick-cooking rolled oats (not instant)	3 cups	750 mL
All-purpose flour	1 1/2 cups	375 mL
Unsweetened medium coconut	1 cup	250 mL
Sultana raisins	1 cup	250 mL
Natural wheat bran	3/4 cup	175 mL
Shelled sunflower seeds	1/2 cup	125 mL
Chopped walnuts (or your favourite)	1/2 cup	125 mL
Baking soda	1 tsp.	5 mL
Salt	1 tsp.	5 mL

Cream margarine and peanut butter in large bowl. Add honey, eggs and vanilla. Beat well.

Add remaining 9 ingredients. Stir well. Roll dough into balls, using 1 tbsp. (15 mL) for each. Flatten slightly. Arrange cookies, about 2 inches (5 cm) apart, on ungreased cookie sheets. Bake in 375°F (190°C) oven for about 12 minutes until golden. Let stand on cookie sheets for 5 minutes before removing to wire racks to cool. Makes 8 dozen (96) cookies.

1 cookie: 74 Calories; 3.5 g Total Fat (1.3 g Mono, 0.9 g Poly, 1.1 g Sat); 4 mg Cholesterol; 10 g Carbohydrate; 1 g Fibre; 2 g Protein; 59 mg Sodium

Pictured on page 49.

Soft Molasses Drops

An old-time recipe. Moist and spicy.

All-purpose flour	3 1/2 cups	875 mL
Granulated sugar	3/4 cup	175 mL
Ground ginger	1 tsp.	5 mL
Ground cinnamon	1 tsp.	5 mL
Salt	1/2 tsp.	2 mL
Fancy (mild) molasses	3/4 cup	175 mL
Hard margarine (or butter), softened	3/4 cup	175 mL
Large egg	1	1
Baking soda	1 1/2 tsp.	7 mL
Hot prepared strong coffee (or hot milk)	1/2 cup	125 mL

Measure first 8 ingredients, in order given, into large bowl. Stir.

Stir baking soda into hot coffee. Add to flour mixture. Beat well. Drop, using 1 tbsp. (15 mL) for each, about 2 inches (5 cm) apart, onto greased cookie sheets. Bake in 375°F (190°C) oven for 10 to 12 minutes until dry but soft. Let stand on cookie sheets for 5 minutes before removing to wire racks to cool. Makes 5 dozen (60) cookies.

1 cookie: 73 Calories; 2.6 g Total Fat (1.6 g Mono, 0.3 g Poly, 0.5 g Sat); 4 mg Cholesterol; 12 g Carbohydrate; trace Fibre; 1 g Protein; 83 mg Sodium

Pictured below.

Left and Top Centre: Soft Molasses Drops, this page
Bottom Centre: Nutri-Cookies, page 48
Right: Hermits, page 50

Hermits

Hard margarine (or butter), softened	1 cup	250 mL
Brown sugar, packed	1 1/2 cups	375 mL
Large eggs	3	3
Vanilla	1 tsp.	5 mL
All-purpose flour	3 cups	750 mL
Sultana raisins	1 cup	250 mL
Chopped pitted dates	1 cup	250 mL
Chopped walnuts (or your favourite)	2/3 cup	150 mL
Baking powder	1 tsp.	5 mL
Baking soda	1 tsp.	5 mL
Ground cinnamon	1 tsp.	5 mL
Ground nutmeg	1/2 tsp.	2 mL
Salt	1/2 tsp.	2 mL
Ground allspice	1/4 tsp.	1 mL

Cream margarine and sugar in large bowl. Add eggs, 1 at a time, beating well after each addition. Add vanilla. Beat.

Add remaining 10 ingredients. Stir until well distributed. Drop, using 1 tbsp. (15 mL) for each, about 2 inches (5 cm) apart, onto greased cookie sheets. Bake in 375°F (190°C) oven for 6 to 8 minutes until golden. Let stand on cookie sheets for 5 minutes before removing to wire racks to cool. Makes 4 1/2 dozen (54) cookies.

1 cookie: 117 Calories; 4.9 g Total Fat (2.7 g Mono, 1 g Poly, 0.9 g Sat); 12 mg Cholesterol; 17 g Carbohydrate; 1 g Fibre; 2 g Protein; 101 mg Sodium

Pictured on page 49.

Butterscotch Cookies

Smooth peanut butter	3 tbsp.	50 mL
Butterscotch chips	1 cup	250 mL
Cornflakes cereal	3 cups	750 mL
Chopped pecans (or walnuts)	1/2 cup	125 mL

These no-bake cookies are golden and crunchy. Sweet, with a mild peanut butter flavour!

Heat peanut butter and chips in large heavy saucepan on lowest heat, stirring often, until chips are almost melted. Do not overheat. Remove from heat. Stir until smooth.

Add cereal and pecans. Stir until coated. Drop, using 2 tbsp. (30 mL) for each, onto waxed paper-lined cookie sheets. Let stand until set. Makes about 2 1/2 dozen (30) cookies.

1 cookie: 53 Calories; 2.4 g Total Fat (1.3 g Mono, 0.6 g Poly, 0.3 g Sat); 0 mg Cholesterol; 8 g Carbohydrate; trace Fibre; 1 g Protein; 36 mg Sodium

Pictured below.

An Italian favourite. This dessert (boh-KOHN-nee DOHL-chay) has meringue layers smothered with chocolate, strawberries and cream.

strawberry meringue shortcake

Trace ten 4 inch (10 cm) circles as directed in recipe. Divide and spoon egg white mixture into circles. Spread evenly to edges, forming raised sides. Bake as directed for about 30 minutes. To serve, fill with sweetened strawberries and top with whipped cream.

Bocconne Dolce

MERINGUE		
Egg whites (large), room temperature	6	6
Cream of tartar	1/4 tsp.	1 mL
Granulated sugar	1 1/2 cups	375 mL
FILLING		
Semi-sweet chocolate chips	1 cup	250 mL
Water	3 tbsp.	50 mL
Whipping cream	3 cups	750 mL
Granulated sugar	1/3 cup	75 mL
Vanilla	2 tsp.	10 mL
Fresh strawberries, sliced lengthwise	3 cups	750 mL

Fresh whole strawberries, for garnish
Chocolate curls (see Note, page 57),
    for garnish

Meringue: Beat egg whites and cream of tartar in medium bowl until soft peaks form. Add sugar, 1 tbsp. (15 mL) at a time while beating, until stiff peaks form and sugar is dissolved. Line bottoms of 2 baking sheets with parchment (not waxed) paper. Trace two 8 inch (20 cm) circles about 1 1/2 inches (3.8 cm) apart on first paper, and one 8 inch (20 cm) circle on second paper. Turn papers over (or use foil with circles marked on top). Divide and spoon meringue onto circles. Spread evenly to edge of each. Bake in 250°F (120°C) oven for about 45 minutes until dry. Turn oven off. Let stand in oven with door ajar until cool. Remove meringues to wire racks and discard parchment paper.

Filling: Heat chips and water in small heavy saucepan on lowest heat, stirring often, until chips are almost melted. Do not overheat. Remove from heat. Stir until smooth. Divide and spread over 2 meringues.

Beat whipping cream, sugar and vanilla in large bowl until stiff peaks form. Divide and spread over all 3 meringues.

Carefully place 1 meringue with chocolate on serving plate. Spoon 1/2 of sliced strawberries evenly over whipped cream. Place second meringue with chocolate on top. Spoon remaining strawberries evenly over whipped cream. Place third meringue on top.

Garnish with strawberries and chocolate curls. Chill for 4 to 5 hours before serving. Serves 8.

1 serving: 612 Calories; 37.2 g Total Fat (11.1 g Mono, 1.3 g Poly, 22.9 g Sat); 110 mg Cholesterol; 70 g Carbohydrate; 3 g Fibre; 6 g Protein; 78 mg Sodium

Pictured on page 53.

Also known as Death By Chocolate, this is a wonderful crowd-pleaser. Recipe can be cut in half for a smaller group.

Truffle Trifle

Box of chocolate cake mix (2 layer size)	1	1
Coffee-flavoured liqueur (such as Kahlúa) or 1/2 cup (125 mL) cold prepared strong coffee	2/3 cup	150 mL
Boxes of instant chocolate pudding powder (4 serving size, each)	2	2
Milk	4 cups	1 L
Frozen whipped topping, thawed	4 cups	1 L
Chocolate-covered crispy toffee bars (such as Heath or Skor), 1 1/2 oz. (39 g) each, crushed	6	6
Chocolate curls (see Note, page 57), for garnish		

Prepare cake mix according to package directions. Divide and spread evenly in 2 greased 8 inch (20 cm) round pans. Bake as directed. Let stand in pans for 5 minutes before inverting onto wire racks to cool completely.

Transfer first cake layer to cutting board. Drizzle with 1/2 of liqueur. Cut into 1 inch (2.5 cm) cubes. Transfer to 6 quart (6 L) glass trifle bowl. Transfer second cake layer to cutting board. Drizzle with remaining liqueur. Cut into 1 inch (2.5 cm) cubes. Set aside.

Beat pudding powder and milk in medium bowl until slightly thickened. Pour 1/2 of pudding over cake in bowl.

Spread 1/2 of whipped topping evenly over pudding. Sprinkle 1/2 of crushed toffee bars over whipped topping. Repeat layering with remaining cake cubes, pudding, whipped topping and crushed toffee bars.

Garnish with chocolate curls. Chill for 1 hour. Serves 20.

1 serving: 303 Calories; 11.2 g Total Fat (1.7 g Mono, 0.4 g Poly, 4.6 g Sat); 9 mg Cholesterol; 45 g Carbohydrate; 0 g Fibre; 4 g Protein; 434 mg Sodium

Pictured on page 55.

Left: Mango Raspberry Trifles, page 56
Right: Truffle Trifle, above

Mango and fresh raspberries make this a very colourful dessert. Assemble in individual wine glasses and serve after a special meal.

Mango Raspberry Trifles

Orange-flavoured liqueur (such as Grand Marnier)	2 tbsp.	30 mL
Orange juice	1/4 cup	60 mL
Mascarpone cheese	1 1/3 cups	325 mL
Icing (confectioner's) sugar	1/3 cup	75 mL
Giant ladyfingers	8	8
Cans of sliced mango with syrup (14 oz., 398 mL, each), drained and sliced diagonally	2	2
Fresh raspberries	1 1/3 cups	325 mL

Combine liqueur and orange juice in small bowl.

Beat mascarpone cheese and icing sugar in separate small bowl until smooth.

Break each ladyfinger in half, for a total of 16 pieces. Dip 8 pieces into orange juice mixture. Place 2 pieces in each of 4 serving glasses. Divide and spoon 1/2 of mango over ladyfingers. Divide and spoon 1/2 of cheese mixture over mango. Divide and spoon 1/2 of raspberries over cheese mixture. Dip remaining ladyfinger pieces in orange juice mixture. Repeat layering with remaining ladyfinger pieces, mango and cheese mixture. Garnish with remaining raspberries. Chill. Serves 4.

1 serving: 560 Calories; 32.1 g Total Fat (9.3 g Mono, 1.7 g Poly, 19 g Sat); 210 mg Cholesterol; 57 g Carbohydrate; 4 g Fibre; 11 g Protein; 293 mg Sodium

Pictured on page 55.

Pure bliss. Soft and creamy. Do not freeze.

Chocolate Mousse

Semi-sweet chocolate chips	1 cup	250 mL
Egg yolks (large)	4	4
Vanilla	1/2 tsp.	2 mL
Egg whites (large), room temperature	4	4
Icing (confectioner's) sugar	1/4 cup	60 mL
Whipping cream (or 1 envelope of dessert topping)	1 cup	250 mL

(continued on next page)

Whipped cream, for garnish
Chocolate filigrees (see Note), for garnish
Chocolate curls (see Note), for garnish

Heat chips in heavy medium saucepan on lowest heat, stirring often, until chips are almost melted. Do not overheat. Remove from heat. Stir until smooth. Add egg yolks and vanilla. Stir well. Transfer to large bowl.

Beat egg whites in medium bowl until soft peaks form. Add icing sugar, 1 tbsp. (15 mL) at a time while beating, until stiff peaks form.

Using same beaters, beat first amount of whipping cream in small bowl until stiff peaks form or prepare dessert topping according to package directions.

Fold 2 tbsp. (30 mL) egg white mixture into chocolate mixture to lighten. Fold in remaining egg white mixture until no white streaks remain. Fold in whipped cream until well combined. Divide and spoon into 8 individual bowls or goblets. Chill for at least 6 hours. Garnish with whipped cream, chocolate filigrees and chocolate curls. Makes 4 3/4 cups (1.2 L) mousse. Serves 8.

1 serving: 255 Calories; 19.3 g Total Fat (6.1 g Mono, 0.9 g Poly, 11 g Sat); 144 mg Cholesterol; 19 g Carbohydrate; 1 g Fibre; 5 g Protein; 45 mg Sodium

Pictured below.

note

To make chocolate filigrees, tape parchment (or waxed) paper onto rolling pin. Drizzle melted chocolate back and forth over curve of rolling pin in desired designs. Let stand until set. Carefully peel paper from chocolate design.

note

To make chocolate curls, peel room temperature chocolate firmly along its length with sharp vegetable peeler. For narrower curls, use flat underside of peeler.

This creamy dish somehow became known as Sex In A Pan—no doubt miscopied from Six in a Pan. Garnish with shaved chocolate.

Six Layer Dessert

CRUST

Hard margarine (or butter)	1/2 cup	125 mL
All-purpose flour	1 cup	250 mL
Finely chopped nuts (your favourite), optional	1/2 cup	125 mL
Granulated sugar	2 tbsp.	30 mL

FILLING

Block of cream cheese, softened	8 oz.	250 g
Icing (confectioner's) sugar	1 cup	250 mL
Whipping cream (or 1 envelope of dessert topping)	1 cup	250 mL
Box of instant chocolate pudding powder (4 serving size)	1	1
Milk	1 1/2 cups	375 mL
Box of instant vanilla pudding powder (4 serving size)	1	1
Milk	1 1/2 cups	375 mL

Crust: Melt margarine in medium saucepan. Remove from heat. Add flour, nuts and sugar. Stir well. Press firmly in ungreased 9 x 13 inch (22 x 33 cm) pan. Bake in 325°F (160°C) oven for about 15 minutes until golden. Let stand in pan on wire rack until cooled completely.

Filling: Beat cream cheese and icing sugar in medium bowl until smooth. Spread evenly over crust.

Beat whipping cream in small bowl until stiff peaks form. Spread 1/2 of whipped cream evenly over cream cheese layer.

Beat chocolate pudding powder and first amount of milk in medium bowl for about 2 minutes until slightly thickened. Spread evenly over whipped cream layer. Let stand until set.

Beat vanilla pudding powder and second amount of milk in medium bowl for about 2 minutes until slightly thickened. Spread evenly over chocolate pudding layer. Let stand until set. Spread remaining whipped cream evenly over vanilla pudding layer. Chill overnight. Cuts into 15 pieces.

1 piece: 309 Calories; 18.4 g Total Fat (7.6 g Mono, 1.1 g Poly, 8.8 g Sat); 40 mg Cholesterol; 33 g Carbohydrate; trace Fibre; 4 g Protein; 352 mg Sodium

Pictured on page 59.

Top: Raspberry Dessert, page 60
Centre: Six Layer Dessert, above
Bottom: Glimmering Slice, page 61

Mix and match various combinations of strawberry or raspberry jelly powder and frozen strawberries or raspberries. All are delicious!

Raspberry Dessert

GRAHAM CRUMB CRUST

Hard margarine (or butter), melted	1/2 cup	125 mL
Graham cracker crumbs	2 cups	500 mL
Brown sugar, packed	1/4 cup	60 mL

SECOND LAYER

Block of cream cheese, softened	8 oz.	250 g
Icing (confectioner's) sugar	1/2 cup	125 mL
Vanilla	1 tsp.	5 mL
Salt	1/2 tsp.	2 mL

THIRD LAYER

Boiling water	1 1/4 cups	300 mL
Boxes of strawberry-flavoured jelly powder (gelatin), 3 oz. (85 g) each	2	2
Granulated sugar	1/4 cup	60 mL
Package of frozen raspberries in syrup, thawed	15 oz.	425 g
Lemon juice	1 tsp.	5 mL

TOP LAYER

Whipping cream	2 cups	500 mL
Icing (confectioner's) sugar	1/4 cup	60 mL
Vanilla	1 tsp.	5 mL

Graham Crumb Crust: Combine margarine, graham crumbs and brown sugar in medium bowl. Stir well. Reserve 1/2 cup (125 mL) crumb mixture for garnish. Press remaining crumb mixture firmly in ungreased 9 x 13 inch (22 x 33 cm) pan. Bake in 350°F (175°C) oven for 10 minutes. Let stand in pan on wire rack until cooled completely.

Second Layer: Beat all 4 ingredients in small bowl until smooth. Spread evenly over graham crust.

Third Layer: Pour boiling water into separate small bowl. Add jelly powder and sugar. Stir until dissolved.

Add raspberries with syrup and lemon juice. Stir. Chill, stirring and scraping side of bowl every 10 minutes, until jelly mixture starts to thicken. Spread evenly over cream cheese layer. Chill until set.

Top Layer: Beat all 3 ingredients in small bowl until stiff peaks form. Spread evenly over jelly layer. Sprinkle with reserved crumbs. Chill. Cuts into 15 pieces.

(continued on next page)

1 piece: 395 Calories; 24.3 g Total Fat (9.6 g Mono, 1.4 g Poly, 12 g Sat); 57 mg Cholesterol; 42 g Carbohydrate; 2 g Fibre; 4 g Protein; 318 mg Sodium

Pictured on page 59.

Glimmering Slice

This looks as spectacular as it tastes!

GRAHAM CRUMB CRUST		
Hard margarine (or butter), melted	1/2 cup	125 mL
Graham cracker crumbs	2 cups	500 mL
Brown sugar, packed	1/4 cup	60 mL
SECOND LAYER		
Envelope of unflavoured gelatin (1 tbsp., 15 mL)	1	1
Cold water	1/4 cup	60 mL
Cold water	1/2 cup	125 mL
Lemon juice	1/2 cup	125 mL
Can of sweetened condensed milk	11 oz.	300 mL
THIRD LAYER		
Boiling water	3 cups	750 mL
Boxes of raspberry-flavoured jelly powder (gelatin), 3 oz. (85 g) each	2	2

Graham Crumb Crust: Combine margarine, graham crumbs and brown sugar in medium bowl. Stir well. Press firmly in ungreased 9 x 13 inch (22 x 33 cm) pan. Bake in 350°F (175°C) oven for 10 minutes. Let stand in pan on wire rack until cooled completely.

Second Layer: Sprinkle gelatin over first amount of cold water in small saucepan. Let stand for 1 minute. Heat and stir on low until gelatin is dissolved. Remove from heat.

Combine second amount of cold water, lemon juice and condensed milk in small bowl. Add gelatin mixture. Beat well. Spread evenly over graham crust.

Third Layer: Pour boiling water into separate small bowl. Add jelly powder. Stir until jelly powder is dissolved. Chill, stirring and scraping side of bowl every 10 minutes, until jelly mixture starts to thicken. Spread evenly over lemon mixture. Chill until set. Cuts into 15 pieces.

1 piece: 254 Calories; 9.9 g Total Fat (5.4 g Mono, 0.9 g Poly, 3 g Sat); 9 mg Cholesterol; 39 g Carbohydrate; trace Fibre; 4 g Protein; 212 mg Sodium

Pictured on page 59.

Top with your favourite fruit to create a colourful presentation.

Fruit Pizza

CRUST

All-purpose flour	1 1/4 cups	300 mL
Brown sugar, packed	1/3 cup	75 mL
Icing (confectioner's) sugar	3 tbsp.	50 mL
Hard margarine (or butter), cut up	2/3 cup	150 mL

TOPPING

Blocks of cream cheese (4 oz., 125 g, each), softened	3	3
Granulated sugar	1/2 cup	125 mL
Vanilla	1 tsp.	5 mL
Variety of fresh fruit (such as strawberries, kiwifruit, peaches and blueberries), sliced		

APRICOT GLAZE

Apricot jam (or orange marmalade)	1/4 cup	60 mL
Water	1 tbsp.	15 mL

Crust: Combine flour, brown sugar and icing sugar in medium bowl. Cut in margarine until mixture resembles fine crumbs. Press mixture together to form smooth ball. Press firmly in ungreased 12 inch (30 cm) pizza pan. Bake in 350°F (175°C) oven for 10 to 15 minutes until golden. Let stand in pan on wire rack until cooled completely.

Topping: Beat cream cheese, sugar and vanilla in large bowl until smooth. Spread evenly over crust. Arrange fruit in attractive pattern over cream cheese mixture.

Apricot Glaze: Combine apricot jam and water in small bowl. Press through sieve into separate small bowl. Brush lightly over fruit. Chill. Cuts into 12 wedges.

1 wedge: 359 Calories; 22 g Total Fat (10.1 g Mono, 1.5 g Poly, 9.1 g Sat); 34 mg Cholesterol; 38 g Carbohydrate; 2 g Fibre; 4 g Protein; 225 mg Sodium

Pictured on page 63.

This scrumptious dessert will catch everyone's attention when you bring it out of the freezer!

Peanut Ice Cream Treat

Butterscotch (or caramel) ice cream topping	1/3 cup	75 mL
Chocolate (or fudge) ice cream topping	1/3 cup	75 mL
Commercial chocolate crumb crust (9 inch, 22 cm, diameter)	1	1
Vanilla (or butterscotch ripple) ice cream, softened	4 cups	1 L
Roasted unsalted peanuts, chopped	1/2 cup	125 mL
Butterscotch (or caramel) ice cream topping, for garnish		
Chocolate (or fudge) ice cream topping, for garnish		

Spoon alternating teaspoonfuls (using 1 tsp., 5 mL, for each) of first amounts of butterscotch and chocolate toppings over crust. Freeze for 20 minutes.

Spread ice cream evenly over crust.

Sprinkle peanuts over ice cream. Cover with plastic wrap. Freeze for at least 8 hours or overnight until firm.

Drizzle second amounts of butterscotch and chocolate toppings over peanuts. Freeze until firm. Cuts into 8 wedges.

1 wedge: 425 Calories; 23.1 g Total Fat (9.2 g Mono, 4.4 g Poly, 8.1 g Sat); 33 mg Cholesterol; 52 g Carbohydrate; 1 g Fibre; 7 g Protein; 313 mg Sodium

Pictured on page 65.

Can it get any better than this for banana split lovers?

note

To toast nuts, place in single layer in ungreased shallow pan. Bake in 350°F (175°C) oven for 5 to 8 minutes, stirring or shaking often, until desired doneness.

chocolate dips

Heat and stir 2 semi-sweet chocolate baking squares (1 oz., 28 g, each) in small heavy saucepan on lowest heat until chocolate is almost melted. Do not overheat. Remove from heat. Stir until smooth. Dip bottom half of each of 18 banana chips in chocolate, allowing excess to drip back into saucepan. Place chips on parchment paper-lined baking sheet. Chill until set. Makes 18 dips.

Banana Macadamia Sundaes

CARAMEL SAUCE

Brown sugar, packed	1/2 cup	125 mL
Hard margarine (or butter)	1/3 cup	75 mL
Whipping cream	1/3 cup	75 mL
Vanilla	1/2 tsp.	2 mL

CHOCOLATE FUDGE SAUCE

Whipping cream	1/2 cup	125 mL
Semi-sweet chocolate bar (3 1/2 oz., 100 g), chopped	1	1
Large marshmallows, chopped	6	6
Chocolate ice cream, approximately	3 cups	750 mL
Medium bananas	6	6
Whipped cream	1 1/2 cups	375 mL
Coarsely chopped macadamia nuts, toasted (see Note)	3/4 cup	175 mL
Chocolate Dips, for garnish	18	18

Caramel Sauce: Heat and stir all 4 ingredients in medium saucepan on medium until boiling. Boil, without stirring, for about 5 minutes until smooth and slightly thickened. Remove from heat. Makes about 2/3 cup (150 mL) Caramel Sauce.

Chocolate Fudge Sauce: Heat and stir whipping cream, chocolate and marshmallow in medium saucepan on medium until smooth. Makes about 1 cup (250 mL) fudge sauce.

In each of six 1 1/2 cup (375 mL) float glasses or wine goblets, layer as follows:

1. 1 scoop ice cream (1/4 cup, 60 mL)
2. 1/2 banana, sliced
3. 1 1/2 tbsp. (25 mL) Caramel Sauce
4. 2 tbsp. (30 mL) whipped cream
5. 1 tbsp. (15 mL) macadamia nuts
6. 1 scoop ice cream (1/4 cup, 60 mL)
7. 1/2 banana, sliced
8. 2 1/2 tbsp. (37 mL) Chocolate Fudge Sauce
9. 2 tbsp. (30 mL) whipped cream
10. 1 tbsp. (15 mL) macadamia nuts

Garnish each with 3 Chocolate Dips. Makes 6 sundaes.

1 sundae: 832 Calories; 56 g Total Fat (25.6 g Mono, 2.4 g Poly, 25 g Sat); 101 mg Cholesterol; 86 g Carbohydrate; 4 g Fibre; 7 g Protein; 217 mg Sodium

Pictured on page 67 and on back cover.

Pears poached in maple syrup and port wine, with a hint of cinnamon and cloves. The perfect treat on a cold day.

Poached Maple Pears

Fresh firm medium pears	4	4
Port wine	1 cup	250 mL
Orange juice	1/2 cup	125 mL
Maple (or maple-flavoured) syrup	1/3 cup	75 mL
Cinnamon stick (4 inch, 10 cm, length)	1	1
Whole cloves	6	6

Fresh mint leaves, for garnish

Carefully remove cores from pears using apple corer, leaving pear whole. Peel pears.

Combine next 5 ingredients in medium saucepan. Lay pears on sides in wine mixture. Bring to a boil on medium. Reduce heat to medium-low. Simmer, uncovered, for 15 to 20 minutes, turning pears occasionally, until softened and evenly coloured. Remove pears using slotted spoon. Cover to keep warm. Remove and discard cinnamon stick and cloves. Bring wine mixture to a boil on medium. Boil, uncovered, for 10 to 15 minutes until reduced to about 3/4 cup (175 mL).

Slice pears evenly, making 6 or 7 cuts from large end of pear to within 1/2 inch (12 mm) of small end. Place 1 pear, large end down, on each of 4 dessert plates. Fan pear slices out slightly. Drizzle with wine mixture. Garnish with mint leaves. Serves 4.

1 serving: 177 Calories; 0.2 g Total Fat (0 g Mono, 0 g Poly, 0 g Sat); 0 mg Cholesterol; 35 g Carbohydrate; 3 g Fibre; 1 g Protein; 9 mg Sodium

Pictured on page 69.

Top Left: Brandied Peaches, page 70
Top Right: Baked Apples, page 70
Centre: Poached Maple Pears, above

Make as many or as few as needed. Good with a scoop of ice cream.

variations

Add 1 tsp. (5 mL) ground cinnamon to brown sugar. Stir well. Proceed as directed.

Remove apples from oven about halfway through baking time. Spoon mincemeat into cavities. Bake as directed.

A dessert solution that fits all occasions.

variation

Use only 2 tbsp. (30 mL) reserved juice and substitute Grand Marnier (orange-flavoured liqueur) for the brandy.

Baked Apples

Medium cooking apples (such as McIntosh)	4	4
Brown sugar, packed	1 cup	250 mL
Hard margarine (or butter), softened	2 tsp.	10 mL

Carefully remove cores from apples using apple corer, leaving apples whole (with peel). Arrange in ungreased 8 x 8 inch (20 x 20 cm) pan. Divide and pack brown sugar into centre of each apple. Spoon 1/2 tsp. (2 mL) margarine over brown sugar. Bake in 350°F (175°C) oven for 25 to 35 minutes until apples are tender. Transfer 1 apple to each of 4 individual bowls. Spoon sauce from pan over apples. Serves 4.

1 serving: 317 Calories; 2.4 g Total Fat (1.3 g Mono, 0.3 g Poly, 0.5 g Sat); 0 mg Cholesterol; 78 g Carbohydrate; 3 g Fibre; 0 g Protein; 45 mg Sodium

Pictured on page 69.

Brandied Peaches

Cans of peach halves in pear juice (14 oz., 398 mL, each)	2	2
Brown sugar, packed	2/3 cup	150 mL
Hard margarine (or butter)	2 tbsp.	30 mL
Ground cinnamon	1/4 tsp.	1 mL
Lemon juice	1 tsp.	5 mL
Brandy flavouring (or 1/4 cup, 60 mL, brandy)	1 tsp.	5 mL
Almond flavouring (optional)	1/4 tsp.	1 mL
Vanilla ice cream	6 cups	1.5 L

Drain peaches, reserving juice. Chop peaches. Transfer to medium saucepan. Add reserved juice. Add next 6 ingredients. Bring to a boil on medium. Reduce heat to medium-low. Simmer, uncovered, for 5 minutes, stirring occasionally.

Scoop 1/2 cup (125 mL) ice cream into each of 12 individual dishes. Divide and spoon brandied peaches over top. Serves 12.

1 serving: 237 Calories; 9.6 g Total Fat (3.5 g Mono, 0.5 g Poly, 5.1 g Sat); 31 mg Cholesterol; 37 g Carbohydrate; 1 g Fibre; 3 g Protein; 86 mg Sodium

Pictured on page 69.

Brown Betty

Peeled, cored and sliced cooking apples (such as McIntosh)	6 cups	1.5 L
Granulated sugar	3/4 cup	175 mL
STREUSEL TOPPING		
All-purpose flour	1 1/4 cups	300 mL
Brown sugar, packed	3/4 cup	175 mL
Salt	1/2 tsp.	2 mL
Hard margarine (or butter), cut up	1/2 cup	125 mL

Place apple slices in ungreased shallow 3 quart (3 L) casserole. Sprinkle sugar over top.

Streusel Topping: Combine flour, brown sugar and salt in medium bowl. Cut in margarine until mixture resembles coarse crumbs. Scatter evenly over apple. Press down lightly. Bake, uncovered, in 375°F (190°C) oven for about 40 minutes until apple is tender. Serves 8.

1 serving: 392 Calories; 12.5 g Total Fat (7.9 g Mono, 1.4 g Poly, 2.6 g Sat); 0 mg Cholesterol; 70 g Carbohydrate; 2 g Fibre; 2 g Protein; 299 mg Sodium

Pictured below.

An all-time favourite. Good hot or cold. Even better served with ice cream.

rhubarb betty

Omit apple and use same amount of sliced fresh or frozen rhubarb, adding 1/2 cup (125 mL) more sugar. Better yet, add a few raisins and omit the extra sugar. Bake as directed.

fresh fruit betty

Omit apple and use fresh peaches, peeled and sliced, or fresh apricots, quartered. Bake as directed.

A treat everyone looks forward to! Freezes well.

Nanaimo Bars

BOTTOM LAYER

Hard margarine (or butter)	1/2 cup	125 mL
Cocoa, sifted if lumpy	1/3 cup	75 mL
Granulated sugar	1/4 cup	60 mL
Large egg, fork-beaten	1	1
Graham cracker crumbs	1 3/4 cups	425 mL
Fine (or medium unsweetened) coconut	3/4 cup	175 mL
Finely chopped walnuts	1/2 cup	125 mL

MIDDLE LAYER

Icing (confectioner's) sugar	2 cups	500 mL
Hard margarine (or butter), softened	1/2 cup	125 mL
Milk	3 tbsp.	50 mL
Vanilla custard powder	2 tbsp.	30 mL

TOP LAYER

Semi-sweet chocolate chips	2/3 cup	150 mL
Hard margarine (or butter)	2 tbsp.	30 mL

Bottom Layer: Heat and stir margarine, cocoa and sugar in heavy medium saucepan on medium-low until smooth. Add egg. Stir until thickened. Remove from heat.

Add graham crumbs, coconut and walnuts. Stir well. Press firmly in ungreased 9 x 9 inch (22 x 22 cm) pan.

Middle Layer: Beat all 4 ingredients in medium bowl until smooth. Spread evenly over bottom layer.

Top Layer: Heat chips and margarine in small heavy saucepan on lowest heat, stirring often, until chips are almost melted. Do not overheat. Remove from heat. Stir until smooth. Cool slightly. Spread evenly over middle layer. Chill until top layer is set. Cuts into 36 squares.

1 square: 153 Calories; 10.1 g Total Fat (4.9 g Mono, 1.4 g Poly, 3.3 g Sat); 9 mg Cholesterol; 16 g Carbohydrate; 1 g Fibre; 2 g Protein; 106 mg Sodium

Pictured on page 73.

Top Left: Mars Bars Squares, page 74
Top Right And Bottom: Nanaimo Bars, above
Centre Right: Chocolate Crisps, page 74

Mars Bars Squares

Mars candy bars (1 3/4 oz., 50 g, each, black and red label), chopped	4	4
Hard margarine (or butter)	1/2 cup	125 mL
Crisp rice cereal	3 cups	750 mL
Semi-sweet chocolate chips	1 cup	250 mL
Hard margarine (or butter)	1/4 cup	60 mL

Heat and stir candy bar pieces and first amount of margarine in large heavy saucepan on low until smooth. Remove from heat.

Add cereal. Stir until coated. Press evenly in greased or foil-lined 9 x 9 inch (22 x 22 cm) pan.

Heat chips and second amount of margarine in small heavy saucepan on lowest heat, stirring often, until chips are melted. Spread evenly over cereal mixture in pan. Chill. Cuts into 36 squares.

1 square: 92 Calories; 6.4 g Total Fat (3.5 g Mono, 0.5 g Poly, 2.1 g Sat); 1 mg Cholesterol; 9 g Carbohydrate; trace Fibre; 1 g Protein; 86 mg Sodium

Pictured on page 73.

Chocolate Crisps

Smooth peanut butter	1 cup	250 mL
Liquid honey	3/4 cup	175 mL
Semi-sweet chocolate chips	1 cup	250 mL
Crisp rice cereal	3 cups	750 mL
Salted peanuts	1 cup	250 mL

Heat peanut butter and honey in large heavy saucepan on lowest heat, stirring often, until melted. Bring to a gentle boil. Remove from heat.

Add chips. Stir until smooth.

Add cereal and peanuts. Stir until coated. Press firmly in greased or foil-lined 9 x 9 inch (22 x 22 cm) pan. Chill until firm. Cuts into 36 squares.

1 square: 130 Calories; 7.5 g Total Fat (3.4 g Mono, 1.8 g Poly, 2 g Sat); 0 mg Cholesterol; 15 g Carbohydrate; 1 g Fibre; 3 g Protein; 96 mg Sodium

Pictured on page 73.

Shortbread

All-purpose flour	2 cups	500 mL
Icing (confectioner's) sugar (see Note)	1/2 cup	125 mL
Butter (not margarine), cut up	1 cup	250 mL

Combine flour and icing sugar in large bowl. Cut in butter until mixture resembles fine crumbs. Press mixture together to form smooth ball. Press evenly in ungreased 9 x 9 inch (22 x 22 cm) pan. Prick entire surface of dough with fork through to bottom of pan. Bake in 300°F (150°C) oven for 50 to 60 minutes until just golden. Let stand in pan on wire rack for 5 minutes. Cuts into 36 squares.

1 square: 81 Calories; 5.5 g Total Fat (1.6 g Mono, 0.2 g Poly, 3.4 g Sat); 15 mg Cholesterol; 7 g Carbohydrate; trace Fibre; 1 g Protein; 55 mg Sodium

Pictured below.

A favourite, no-fail recipe for shortbread.

scotch shortbread

Omit icing sugar. Use same amount of granulated sugar.

The perfect ending to an evening meal.

Midnight Mints

BOTTOM LAYER

Hard margarine (or butter)	1/2 cup	125 mL
Cocoa, sifted if lumpy	1/3 cup	75 mL
Granulated sugar	1/4 cup	60 mL
Large egg, fork-beaten	1	1
Graham cracker crumbs	1 3/4 cups	425 mL
Fine coconut	3/4 cup	175 mL
Finely chopped walnuts	1/2 cup	125 mL

MIDDLE LAYER

Icing (confectioner's) sugar	2 cups	500 mL
Hard margarine (or butter), softened	1/3 cup	75 mL
Milk	3 tbsp.	50 mL
Peppermint flavouring	1 tsp.	5 mL
Green liquid (or paste) food colouring		

TOP LAYER

Semi-sweet chocolate chips	2/3 cup	150 mL
Hard margarine (or butter)	2 tbsp.	30 mL

Bottom Layer: Heat and stir margarine, cocoa and sugar in large heavy saucepan on medium until boiling. Reduce heat to medium-low. Add egg. Stir until thickened. Remove from heat.

Add graham crumbs, coconut and walnuts. Stir well. Press firmly in ungreased 9 x 9 inch (22 x 22 cm) pan.

Middle Layer: Beat first 4 ingredients in medium bowl until smooth, adding more milk or icing sugar as necessary until spreading consistency. Add enough food colouring until pale green. Spread evenly over bottom layer.

Top Layer: Heat chips and margarine in small heavy saucepan on lowest heat, stirring often, until chips are almost melted. Do not overheat. Remove from heat. Stir until smooth. Cool slightly. Spread evenly over middle layer. Chill until top layer is set. Cuts into 36 squares.

1 square: 142 Calories; 9.1 g Total Fat (4.3 g Mono, 1.3 g Poly, 3.1 g Sat); 6 mg Cholesterol; 15 g Carbohydrate; 1 g Fibre; 1 g Protein; 90 mg Sodium

Pictured on page 77.

Millionaire means rich—exactly what these squares are!

Millionaire Squares

BOTTOM LAYER		
Hard margarine (or butter)	1/2 cup	125 mL
Finely crushed crisp oatmeal cookies (such as Dad's)	2 cups	500 mL
FILLING		
Semi-sweet chocolate baking squares (1 oz., 28 g, each), chopped (or 1/2 cup, 125 mL, chocolate chips)	3	3
Hard margarine (or butter)	1/2 cup	125 mL
Large egg	1	1
Icing (confectioner's) sugar	2 cups	500 mL
Chopped walnuts (optional)	1/2 cup	125 mL

Bottom Layer: Melt margarine in medium saucepan. Remove from heat. Add crushed cookies. Stir well. Reserve 1/4 cup (60 mL) crumb mixture for topping. Press remaining mixture firmly in greased 8 x 8 inch (20 x 20 cm) pan. Bake in 350°F (175°C) oven for 5 minutes. Let stand in pan on wire rack until cooled completely.

Filling: Heat chocolate and margarine in heavy medium saucepan on lowest heat, stirring often, until chocolate is almost melted. Do not overheat. Remove from heat. Stir until smooth. Add egg. Beat. Add icing sugar, 2 tbsp. (30 mL) at a time while beating, until smooth, adding more icing sugar as necessary until spreading consistency.

Add walnuts. Stir. Spread evenly over bottom layer. Sprinkle reserved crumb mixture over top. Chill until firm. Cuts into 25 squares.

1 square: 169 Calories; 10.6 g Total Fat (6.4 g Mono, 1.1 g Poly, 2.5 g Sat); 9 mg Cholesterol; 19 g Carbohydrate; trace Fibre; 1 g Protein; 129 mg Sodium

Pictured on page 79.

Top Left: Fudgy Macaroons, page 80
Top Right: Millionaire Squares, above
Bottom Right: Butterscotch Confetti, page 81
Bottom Left: Swirl Squares, page 80

The swirl is made with chocolate chips. No need to ice these. The recipe is easily doubled.

variation

Omit the chocolate chips. Cool squares completely. Spread with your favourite icing.

Swirl Squares

Hard margarine (or butter), softened	1/2 cup	125 mL
Brown sugar, packed	1/2 cup	125 mL
Granulated sugar	1/4 cup	60 mL
Vanilla	1/2 tsp.	2 mL
Large egg	1	1
All-purpose flour	1 1/8 cups	280 mL
Baking soda	1/2 tsp.	2 mL
Salt	1/2 tsp.	2 mL
Chopped walnuts	1/2 cup	125 mL
Semi-sweet chocolate chips	1 cup	250 mL

Beat first 5 ingredients in large bowl until light and creamy.

Combine flour, baking soda and salt in small bowl. Add to margarine mixture. Stir until smooth.

Add walnuts. Stir. Spread evenly in greased 9 x 9 inch (22 x 22 cm) pan.

Scatter chips over top. Bake in 375°F (190°C) oven for 1 to 2 minutes until chips are very soft. Remove from oven. Swirl knife through batter to create marble effect. Return to oven. Bake for about 20 minutes until firm and wooden pick inserted in centre comes out clean. Let stand in pan on wire rack until cool. Cuts into 36 squares.

1 square: 94 Calories; 5.4 g Total Fat (2.5 g Mono, 1 g Poly, 1.5 g Sat); 6 mg Cholesterol; 11 g Carbohydrate; 1 g Fibre; 1 g Protein; 86 mg Sodium

Pictured on page 79.

Crunchy butterscotch treats. Similar taste to brown sugar fudge.

Fudgy Macaroons

Granulated sugar	1 1/2 cups	375 mL
Evaporated milk	1 cup	250 mL
Hard margarine (or butter)	1/4 cup	60 mL
Butterscotch chips	2 cups	500 mL
Vanilla	1 tsp.	5 mL

(continued on next page)

Cornflakes cereal, lightly packed	4 cups	1 L
Medium unsweetened coconut	2 1/2 cups	625 mL
Chopped walnuts	1 cup	250 mL

Heat and stir sugar, evaporated milk and margarine in large heavy saucepan on medium. Bring to a rolling boil. Immediately remove from heat.

Add chips and vanilla. Stir until smooth.

Add cereal, coconut and walnuts. Stir until coated. Press firmly in greased or foil-lined 9 x 9 inch (20 x 20 cm) pan. Chill until firm. Cuts into 36 squares.

1 square: 198 Calories; 8.6 g Total Fat (1.8 g Mono, 1.6 g Poly, 4.6 g Sat); 3 mg Cholesterol; 29 g Carbohydrate; 1 g Fibre; 3 g Protein; 138 mg Sodium

Pictured on page 79.

Butterscotch Confetti

Butterscotch chips	1 cup	250 mL
Smooth peanut butter	1/2 cup	125 mL
Hard margarine (or butter)	1/4 cup	60 mL
Package of miniature multi-coloured marshmallows	8 oz.	250 g

Heat first 3 ingredients in large heavy saucepan on lowest heat, stirring often, until chips are almost melted. Do not overheat. Remove from heat. Stir until smooth. Let stand until bottom of saucepan is cool enough to touch.

Add marshmallows. Stir until coated. Press firmly in greased or foil-lined 9 x 9 inch (22 x 22 cm) pan. Chill until firm. Cuts into 36 squares.

1 square: 73 Calories; 3.4 g Total Fat (1.8 g Mono, 0.7 g Poly, 0.7 g Sat); 0 mg Cholesterol; 10 g Carbohydrate; trace Fibre; 1 g Protein; 39 mg Sodium

Pictured on page 79.

There is no excuse not to have this treat on hand. Freezes well. Colourful!

variation

Line bottom of pan with whole graham crackers first. Proceed as directed in recipe.

variation

Add 1/2 cup (125 mL) chopped walnuts and/or 1/2 cup (125 mL) medium unsweetened coconut to recipe ingredients.

Make these when you're looking for something a little different.

Tweed Squares

Hard margarine (or butter), softened	1/2 cup	125 mL
Granulated sugar	2/3 cup	150 mL
All-purpose flour	1 1/3 cups	325 mL
Baking powder	2 tsp.	10 mL
Salt	1/2 tsp.	2 mL
Milk	1/2 cup	125 mL
Egg whites (large), room temperature	2	2
Semi-sweet chocolate baking squares (1 oz., 28 g, each), finely grated	2	2
VANILLA ICING		
Icing (confectioner's) sugar	1 1/2 cups	375 mL
Hard margarine (or butter), softened	3 tbsp.	50 mL
Water	1 1/2 tbsp.	25 mL
Vanilla	1/2 tsp.	2 mL
Semi-sweet chocolate baking squares (1 oz., 28 g, each), chopped	2	2
Hard margarine (or butter)	1 tbsp.	15 mL

Beat margarine and sugar in large bowl until light and creamy.

Combine flour, baking powder and salt in small bowl. Add flour mixture to margarine mixture in 2 additions, alternating with milk in 1 addition, beginning and ending with flour mixture.

Beat egg whites in separate small bowl until stiff peaks form. Fold into batter until no white streaks remain.

Fold in grated chocolate. Spread evenly in greased 9 x 9 inch (22 x 22 cm) pan. Bake in 350°F (175°C) oven for about 35 minutes until golden. Let stand in pan on wire rack until cooled completely.

Vanilla Icing: Beat first 4 ingredients in small bowl until smooth, adding more water or icing sugar as necessary until spreading consistency. Spread evenly over first layer. Let stand for at least 1 hour until set.

(continued on next page)

Heat chocolate and margarine in small heavy saucepan on lowest heat, stirring often, until chocolate is almost melted. Do not overheat. Remove from heat. Stir until smooth. Cool slightly. Spread evenly over icing. Chill until top layer is set. Cuts into 36 squares.

1 square: 107 Calories; 5 g Total Fat (2.9 g Mono, 0.4 g Poly, 1.4 g Sat); 0 mg Cholesterol; 15 g Carbohydrate; trace Fibre; 1 g Protein; 105 mg Sodium

Pictured below.

Top: Tweed Squares, page 82
Bottom: Chocolate Roll, page 84

A colourful confection with a smooth texture. After a few slices are cut, you can pop it back in the refrigerator or freezer.

variation

Reduce coconut to 1/4 cup (60 mL). Add with rest of ingredients. Mix well. Press firmly in greased or foil-lined 8 x 8 inch (20 x 20 cm) pan. Cuts into 25 squares.

Chocolate Roll

Semi-sweet chocolate chips	1 cup	250 mL
Hard margarine (or butter)	2 tbsp.	30 mL
Miniature multi-coloured marshmallows	2 1/2 cups	625 mL
Icing (confectioner's) sugar	1 cup	250 mL
Quartered maraschino cherries, well-drained	1/2 cup	125 mL
Chopped walnuts	1/2 cup	125 mL
Large egg, fork-beaten	1	1
Medium unsweetened coconut	1/2 cup	125 mL

Heat chips and margarine in large heavy saucepan on lowest heat, stirring often, until chips are almost melted. Do not overheat. Remove from heat. Stir until smooth.

Add next 5 ingredients. Stir well. Let stand until cool enough to handle. Shape mixture into 2 1/2 inch (6.4 cm) diameter log.

Sprinkle coconut on waxed paper on work surface. Roll log in coconut until coated. Wrap in waxed paper or plastic wrap. Chill until firm. Cut into 1/2 inch (12 mm) slices, cleaning knife under hot water after each slice. Cuts into 24 slices.

1 slice: 116 Calories; 6.3 g Total Fat (1.9 g Mono, 1.2 g Poly, 2.8 g Sat); 9 mg Cholesterol; 16 g Carbohydrate; 1 g Fibre; 1 g Protein; 18 mg Sodium

Pictured on page 83.

A light, summer treat. Freezes well so you can pull one out whenever you get a craving.

Lemon Bars

BOTTOM LAYER

All-purpose flour	2 cups	500 mL
Icing (confectioner's) sugar	3/4 cup	175 mL
Hard margarine (or butter), softened, cut up	1 cup	250 mL

TOP LAYER

Large eggs	4	4
Lemon juice	1/3 cup	75 mL
Grated lemon peel	1 tbsp.	15 mL

(continued on next page)

Granulated sugar	1 1/2 cups	375 mL
All-purpose flour	1/4 cup	60 mL
Baking powder	1 tsp.	5 mL

Icing (confectioner's) sugar, for dusting

Bottom Layer: Combine flour and icing sugar in medium bowl. Cut in margarine until mixture resembles fine crumbs. Press firmly in ungreased 9 x 13 inch (22 x 33 cm) pan. Bake in 350°F (175°C) oven for about 20 minutes until golden. Remove from oven.

Top Layer: Beat eggs in large bowl until frothy. Add lemon juice and peel. Stir.

Combine granulated sugar, flour and baking powder in small bowl. Add to egg mixture. Stir until just moistened. Spread evenly over bottom layer. Bake for about 25 minutes until set. Let stand in pan on wire rack for 5 minutes.

Dust evenly with icing sugar using sieve. Let stand until cool. Cuts into 48 bars.

1 bar: 100 Calories; 4.5 g Total Fat (2.8 g Mono, 0.5 g Poly, 1 g Sat); 18 mg Cholesterol; 14 g Carbohydrate; trace Fibre; 1 g Protein; 60 mg Sodium

Pictured below.

Favourite date squares that are not as messy to eat as some others. These crumbs hold together well.

Matrimonial Squares

CRUMB LAYERS

Rolled oats (not instant)	1 1/2 cups	375 mL
All-purpose flour	1 1/4 cups	300 mL
Brown sugar, packed	1 cup	250 mL
Baking soda	1 tsp.	5 mL
Salt	1/2 tsp.	2 mL
Hard margarine (or butter), softened, cut up	1 cup	250 mL

DATE FILLING

Chopped pitted dates	1 1/2 cups	375 mL
Water	2/3 cup	150 mL
Granulated sugar	1/2 cup	125 mL

Crumb Layers: Combine first 5 ingredients in large bowl. Cut in margarine until mixture resembles very coarse crumbs. Press slightly more than 1/2 of mixture firmly in greased 9 x 9 inch (22 x 22 cm) pan. Set remaining mixture aside.

Date Filling: Combine dates, water and sugar in medium saucepan. Bring to a boil on medium. Reduce heat to medium-low. Simmer, uncovered, for about 10 minutes until dates are softened and water is almost evaporated, adding more water if necessary while simmering to soften dates. Spread evenly over bottom layer of crumbs. Sprinkle remaining crumb mixture evenly over top. Press down lightly. Bake in 350°F (175°C) oven for about 30 minutes until golden. Let stand in pan on wire rack until cool. Cuts into 36 squares.

1 square: 139 Calories; 5.7 g Total Fat (3.6 g Mono, 0.7 g Poly, 1.2 g Sat); 0 mg Cholesterol; 21 g Carbohydrate; 1 g Fibre; 1 g Protein; 134 mg Sodium

Pictured on page 87.

Top Right: Cherry Squares, page 88
Bottom Left: Matrimonial Squares, above

This is one of our most popular bar cookies. After you've tried a piece, you'll understand why.

Cherry Squares

BOTTOM LAYER

All-purpose flour	1 1/4 cups	300 mL
Brown sugar, packed	1/3 cup	75 mL
Hard margarine (or butter), softened, cut up	1/2 cup	125 mL

SECOND LAYER

Large eggs	2	2
Brown sugar, packed	1 1/4 cups	300 mL
All-purpose flour	1 tbsp.	15 mL
Baking powder	1/2 tsp.	2 mL
Salt	1/8 tsp.	0.5 mL
Medium unsweetened coconut	1 cup	250 mL
Chopped walnuts	1/2 cup	125 mL
Chopped red glazed cherries (or maraschino cherries, blotted dry)	1/2 cup	125 mL

VANILLA ICING

Icing (confectioner's) sugar	2 cups	500 mL
Hard margarine (or butter), softened	1/4 cup	60 mL
Milk (or water)	2 tbsp.	30 mL
Vanilla	1 tsp.	5 mL

Bottom Layer: Combine flour and brown sugar in small bowl. Cut in margarine until mixture resembles fine crumbs. Press firmly in ungreased 9 x 9 inch (22 x 22 cm) pan. Bake in 350°F (175°C) oven for 15 minutes. Remove from oven.

Second Layer: Beat eggs in medium bowl until frothy. Add remaining ingredients, in order given, stirring after each addition. Spread evenly over bottom layer. Bake for about 25 minutes until golden. Let stand in pan on wire rack until cooled completely.

Vanilla Icing: Beat all 4 ingredients in small bowl until smooth, adding more milk or icing sugar as necessary until spreading consistency. Spread evenly over second layer. Cuts into 36 squares.

1 square: 141 Calories; 6.4 g Total Fat (2.6 g Mono, 1.1 g Poly, 2.4 g Sat); 12 mg Cholesterol; 20 g Carbohydrate; trace Fibre; 2 g Protein; 62 mg Sodium

Pictured on page 87.

Apricot Zings

A long-time favourite. Great to make ahead and freeze. Perfect choice for a bake sale.

BOTTOM LAYER

Graham cracker crumbs	1 cup	250 mL
All-purpose flour	1 cup	250 mL
Brown sugar, packed	1 cup	250 mL
Hard margarine (or butter), melted	3/4 cup	175 mL
Medium unsweetened coconut	1/2 cup	125 mL
Salt	1/2 tsp.	2 mL

APRICOT FILLING

Dried apricots	1 cup	250 mL
Water		
Large eggs	2	2
Brown sugar, packed	1 cup	250 mL
Lemon juice	1 tbsp.	15 mL
All-purpose flour	1/3 cup	75 mL
Baking powder	1/2 tsp.	2 mL
Salt	1/4 tsp.	1 mL

Bottom Layer: Combine first 6 ingredients in medium bowl. Reserve 1 cup (250 mL) crumb mixture. Press remaining mixture firmly in ungreased 9 x 9 inch (22 x 22 cm) pan. Bake in 350°F (175°C) oven for 10 minutes. Remove from oven.

Apricot Filling: Place apricots in small saucepan. Add enough water to cover. Bring to a boil on medium. Reduce heat to medium-low. Simmer, uncovered, for about 15 minutes until apricots are softened. Drain well. Chop.

Beat eggs in medium bowl until frothy. Add brown sugar and lemon juice. Stir well.

Combine flour, baking powder and salt in small bowl. Add to egg mixture. Stir. Add apricots. Stir well. Spread evenly over bottom layer. Sprinkle with reserved crumbs. Bake for 30 to 35 minutes until golden. Let stand in pan on wire rack until cool. Cuts into 36 squares.

1 square: 135 Calories; 5.5 g Total Fat (2.9 g Mono, 0.5 g Poly, 1.7 g Sat); 12 mg Cholesterol; 21 g Carbohydrate; 1 g Fibre; 1 g Protein; 126 mg Sodium

Pictured on page 91.

Using soda crackers in this square gives it a bit of a different touch.

Lemon Crunch

BOTTOM LAYER

Crushed soda crackers	1 1/3 cups	325 mL
Hard margarine (or butter), softened	3/4 cup	175 mL
All-purpose flour	3/4 cup	175 mL
Granulated sugar	1/2 cup	125 mL
Medium unsweetened coconut	1/2 cup	125 mL
Baking powder	1 tsp.	5 mL

LEMON FILLING

Large eggs	3	3
Granulated sugar	1 cup	250 mL
Lemon, grated peel and juice	1	1
Hard margarine (or butter)	1/4 cup	60 mL

Bottom Layer: Combine all 6 ingredients in medium bowl until crumbly. Reserve 1 cup (250 mL) for topping. Press remaining crumb mixture firmly in ungreased 9 x 9 inch (22 x 22 cm) pan. Bake in 350°F (175°C) oven for 15 minutes. Remove from oven.

Lemon Filling: Beat eggs in heavy medium saucepan or top of double boiler. Add remaining 3 ingredients. Heat and stir on medium until thickened. Spread evenly over crumb layer in pan. Sprinkle reserved crumb mixture over top. Bake for about 20 minutes until golden brown. Let stand in pan on wire rack until cool. Cuts into 36 squares.

1 square: 122 Calories; 7.1 g Total Fat (3.9 g Mono, 0.7 g Poly, 2.1 g Sat); 18 mg Cholesterol; 14 g Carbohydrate; trace Fibre; 1 g Protein; 120 mg Sodium

Pictured on page 91.

Left: Apricot Zings, page 89
Right: Lemon Crunch, above

Tastes like a famous candy bar.

Candy Bar Squares

Semi-sweet chocolate chips	2 cups	500 mL
Peanut butter chips	1 cup	250 mL
Granulated sugar	1 1/4 cups	300 mL
Hard margarine (or butter)	1/3 cup	75 mL
Milk	1/3 cup	75 mL
Coarsely chopped salted peanuts	1/4 cup	60 mL
Smooth peanut butter	1/4 cup	60 mL
Marshmallow creme	1 cup	250 mL
Vanilla	1 tsp.	5 mL
Coarsely chopped salted peanuts	3/4 cup	175 mL
Caramels	40	40
Water	2 1/2 tbsp.	37 mL

Heat both chips in large heavy saucepan on lowest heat, stirring often, until chips are almost melted. Do not overheat. Remove from heat. Stir until smooth. Spread about 1/2 of mixture evenly in greased or foil-lined 9 × 13 inch (22 × 33 cm) pan. Let stand until firm.

Heat and stir sugar, margarine and milk in heavy medium saucepan on medium until boiling. Boil for 5 minutes, stirring often. Spread evenly over chip layer.

Sprinkle first amount of peanuts over top.

Heat and stir peanut butter in small heavy saucepan on lowest heat until melted. Remove from heat. Add marshmallow creme and vanilla. Stir until smooth. Spoon mixture in dabs, using 1 tsp. (5 mL) for each, over peanuts.

Sprinkle second amount of peanuts over top.

Heat and stir caramels and water in heavy medium saucepan on lowest heat until smooth. Spread evenly over peanuts. Reheat remaining 1/2 of chip mixture if necessary until spreading consistency. Spread evenly over caramel. Chill until firm. Cuts into 54 squares.

1 square: 139 Calories; 6.7 g Total Fat (2.8 g Mono, 1 g Poly, 2.6 g Sat); 0 mg Cholesterol; 20 g Carbohydrate; 1 g Fibre; 2 g Protein; 70 mg Sodium

Pictured on page 93 and on front cover.

When unexpected company calls, whip these up. They're ready in a flash—and will be eaten just as quickly.

Chocolate Cherry Slice

BOTTOM LAYER

Sweet chocolate baking squares (1 oz., 28 g, each), or 1 1/3 cups (325 mL) chocolate chips	8	8

TOP LAYER

Large eggs	2	2
Granulated sugar	1/2 cup	125 mL
Medium unsweetened coconut	1 1/2 cups	375 mL
Chopped glazed cherries	1/4 cup	60 mL

Icing (confectioner's) sugar, for dusting (optional)

Bottom Layer: Heat chocolate in small heavy saucepan on lowest heat, stirring often, until almost melted. Do not overheat. Remove from heat. Stir until smooth. Spread evenly in bottom of greased 8 × 8 inch (20 × 20 cm) pan. Chill until firm.

Top Layer: Beat eggs and sugar in medium bowl until thick and pale. Add coconut and cherries. Stir. Spread evenly over bottom layer. Bake in 350°F (175°C) oven for 25 to 30 minutes until golden and firm to the touch. Let stand in pan on wire rack until cool. Cover and store in refrigerator.

Just before serving, dust with icing sugar using a sieve. Cuts into 25 squares.

1 square: 112 Calories; 7.2 g Total Fat (1.3 g Mono, 0.2 g Poly, 5.2 g Sat); 17 mg Cholesterol; 13 g Carbohydrate; trace Fibre; 1 g Protein; 9 mg Sodium

Pictured on page 95.

1. Saucepan Brownies, page 97
2. Chocolate Cherry Slice, above
3. Cream Cheese Brownies, page 96

These are fussy to prepare, but are worth the extra time it takes. Very attractive.

variation

Omit the icing. They're delicious uniced.

Cream Cheese Brownies

CHEESE LAYER

Block of cream cheese, softened	4 oz.	125 g
Large egg	1	1
Granulated sugar	1/2 cup	125 mL
All-purpose flour	2 tbsp.	30 mL
Chopped maraschino cherries, well-drained	1/2 cup	125 mL

BROWNIE LAYER

Large eggs	2	2
Granulated sugar	1 cup	250 mL
All-purpose flour	3/4 cup	175 mL
Chopped walnuts	1/2 cup	125 mL
Salt	1/8 tsp.	0.5 mL
Hard margarine (or butter), cut up	1/2 cup	125 mL
Cocoa, sifted if lumpy	1/4 cup	60 mL

CHOCOLATE COFFEE ICING

Icing (confectioner's) sugar	1 1/3 cups	325 mL
Cocoa, sifted if lumpy	1/3 cup	75 mL
Hard margarine (or butter), softened	3 tbsp.	50 mL
Hot prepared strong coffee (or hot water)	1 1/2 tbsp.	25 mL

Cheese Layer: Beat cream cheese and egg in medium bowl until smooth. Combine sugar and flour in small bowl. Add to cream cheese mixture, 2 tbsp. (30 mL) at a time while beating, until smooth. Add cherries. Stir. Set aside.

Brownie Layer: Beat eggs in separate medium bowl until frothy. Add next 4 ingredients. Stir.

Heat and stir margarine and cocoa in small heavy saucepan on lowest heat until smooth. Add to egg mixture. Stir well. Spread about 2/3 of brownie mixture evenly in greased 9 x 9 inch (22 x 22 cm) pan. Spoon mounds of cream cheese mixture, using 1 tbsp. (15 mL) for each, over brownie layer. Spoon remaining brownie mixture in dabs, using 1/2 tsp. (2 mL) for each, over top. Mixtures will look patchy in pan. Bake in 350°F (175°C) oven for 30 to 35 minutes until edges pull away from sides of pan. Let stand in pan on wire rack until cooled completely.

(continued on next page)

Chocolate Coffee Icing: Beat all 4 ingredients in small bowl until smooth, adding more coffee or icing sugar as necessary until spreading consistency. Spread evenly over brownie layer. Cuts into 25 squares.

1 square: 189 Calories; 9.4 g Total Fat (4.6 g Mono, 1.7 g Poly, 2.6 g Sat); 31 mg Cholesterol; 25 g Carbohydrate; 1 g Fibre; 3 g Protein; 97 mg Sodium

Pictured on page 95.

Saucepan Brownies

A no-bake brownie with rich chocolate flavour.

Semi-sweet chocolate chips	2 2/3 cups	650 mL
Evaporated milk	1 cup	250 mL
Vanilla wafer crumbs	3 cups	750 mL
Miniature marshmallows	2 cups	500 mL
Chopped walnuts	1 cup	250 mL
Icing (confectioner's) sugar	1 cup	250 mL
Salt	1/2 tsp.	2 mL
Evaporated milk	2 tsp.	10 mL

Heat and stir chips and first amount of evaporated milk in large heavy saucepan on medium-low until smooth. Do not overheat. Remove from heat. Reserve 1/2 cup (125 mL) chocolate mixture. Set aside.

Add next 5 ingredients to remaining chocolate mixture. Stir well. Press firmly in greased or foil-lined 9 x 9 inch (22 x 22 cm) pan.

Add second amount of evaporated milk to reserved chocolate mixture. Stir well. Spread evenly over crumb mixture. Chill until firm. Cuts into 36 squares.

1 square: 149 Calories; 7.7 g Total Fat (2.4 g Mono, 1.8 g Poly, 3.1 g Sat); 6 mg Cholesterol; 20 g Carbohydrate; 1 g Fibre; 2 g Protein; 66 mg Sodium

Pictured on page 95.

These do melt in your mouth.

Chocolate Coconut Melts

Can of sweetened condensed milk	11 oz.	300 mL
Unsweetened chocolate baking squares (1 oz., 28 g, each), chopped	2	2
Salt	1/4 tsp.	1 mL
Flake coconut	2 2/3 cups	650 mL
Vanilla	1 tsp.	5 mL

Heat and stir condensed milk, chocolate and salt in heavy medium saucepan on medium-low until smooth. Remove from heat.

Add coconut and vanilla. Stir well. Spread evenly in greased 8 x 8 inch (20 x 20 cm) pan. Bake in 350°F (175°C) oven for about 20 minutes until set. Let stand in pan on wire rack until cool. Cuts into 25 squares.

1 square: 129 Calories; 9.1 g Total Fat (1.1 g Mono, 0.2 g Poly, 7.4 g Sat); 5 mg Cholesterol; 12 g Carbohydrate; 1 g Fibre; 2 g Protein; 48 mg Sodium

Pictured on page 99.

You'll need two pans to make these. Wrap individual bars in plastic wrap for an easy take-along breakfast when you roll out of bed and have to run out the door!

note

To toast seeds, place in single layer in ungreased shallow pan. Bake in 350°F (175°C) oven for 5 to 8 minutes, stirring or shaking often, until desired doneness.

Take-Along Breakfast Bars

Quick-cooking rolled oats (not instant)	4 cups	1 L
Medium unsweetened coconut	2 cups	500 mL
Lightly crushed cornflakes cereal	1 cup	250 mL
Chopped dried apricots	1 cup	250 mL
Raisins	1 cup	250 mL
Shelled sunflower seeds, toasted (see Note)	2/3 cup	150 mL
Hard margarine (or butter)	1/2 cup	125 mL
Can of sweetened condensed milk	11 oz.	300 mL
Golden corn syrup	1/4 cup	60 mL
Frozen concentrated orange juice	2 tbsp.	30 mL

(continued on next page)

Combine first 6 ingredients in large bowl.

Melt margarine in medium saucepan. Add remaining 3 ingredients. Heat and stir on low until smooth. Slowly pour into rolled oat mixture while stirring until well combined. Mixture will be sticky. Divide and press firmly in 2 greased 9 × 13 inch (22 × 33 cm) pans. Bake in 325°F (160°C) oven for 20 to 30 minutes until edges are golden. Let stand in pans on wire racks for 5 minutes. Score top of each into 2 × 3 inch (5 × 7.5 cm) bars with knife. Let stand until cool. Each pan cuts into 18 bars, for a total of 36 bars.

1 bar: 197 Calories; 9.4 g Total Fat (2.7 g Mono, 1.6 g Poly, 4.5 g Sat); 4 mg Cholesterol; 26 g Carbohydrate; 2 g Fibre; 4 g Protein; 79 mg Sodium

Pictured below.

Top: Take-Along Breakfast Bars, page 98
Bottom: Chocolate Coconut Melts, page 98

take-along breakfast cookies

Roll out mixture between 2 sheets of greased waxed paper to 1/2 inch (12 mm) thickness. Cut into shapes with cookie cutter. Carefully transfer to greased cookie sheets. Bake in 325°F (160°C) oven for 15 to 20 minutes until edges are golden. Let stand on sheets for 5 minutes before removing to wire racks to cool. Makes about 24 cookies.

Brittle lovers take note: lots of peanuts covered in chocolate. A dream come true!

Chocolate Brittle

Granulated sugar	1 cup	250 mL
White corn syrup	1/2 cup	125 mL
Roasted salted peanuts	1 cup	250 mL
Hard margarine (or butter)	2 tbsp.	30 mL
Vanilla	1 tsp.	5 mL
Baking soda	1 1/2 tsp.	7 mL
TOPPING		
Semi-sweet chocolate chips	3/4 cup	175 mL
Chopped unsalted peanuts	1/3 cup	75 mL

Combine sugar and corn syrup in ungreased 2 quart (2 L) casserole. Microwave, uncovered, on high (100%) for about 4 minutes until sugar is dissolved and mixture is bubbling.

Add peanuts. Stir. Microwave, uncovered, on high (100%) for about 6 minutes, checking at 1 minute intervals, until golden.

Add margarine and vanilla. Stir. Microwave, uncovered, on high (100%) for 1 minute. Stir.

Add baking soda. Stir. Mixture will foam. Immediately turn out onto greased baking sheet with sides. Spread evenly into thin layer.

Topping: Sprinkle chips over hot peanut mixture. Let stand until chips are softened. Spread evenly. Sprinkle with chopped peanuts. Chill until set. Break into irregular-shaped pieces, about 1 1/2 x 2 inches (3.8 x 5 cm) each. Makes about 1 1/4 lbs. (560 g), or about 30 pieces.

1 piece: 114 Calories; 5.5 g Total Fat (2.6 g Mono, 1.2 g Poly, 1.4 g Sat); 0 mg Cholesterol; 16 g Carbohydrate; 1 g Fibre; 2 g Protein; 120 mg Sodium

Pictured on page 101.

Top Left: Chocolate Nuts, page 102
Top Right: Chocolate Marshmallows, page 102
Bottom: Chocolate Brittle, above

These are a pleasant change from the usual mixed nut offering.

Chocolate Nuts

Pecan halves	1 cup	250 mL
Walnut halves	1 cup	250 mL
Chocolate syrup	1/2 cup	125 mL
Cooking oil	4 tsp.	20 mL

Measure pecans and walnuts into medium bowl. Add chocolate syrup and cooking oil. Stir until nuts are well coated. Spread evenly in greased baking sheet with sides. Bake in 350°F (175°C) oven for 8 to 10 minutes, stirring halfway through baking time, until dry and crisp. Makes 2 cups (500 mL).

2 tbsp. (30 mL): 117 Calories; 9.7 g Total Fat (4.5 g Mono, 4 g Poly, 0.9 g Sat); 0 mg Cholesterol; 8 g Carbohydrate; 1 g Fibre; 2 g Protein; 10 mg Sodium

Pictured on page 101.

Allow extra time for this impressive-looking candy dessert. Certainly worth the effort.

note

To toast nuts, place in single layer in ungreased shallow pan. Bake in 350°F (175°C) oven for 5 to 8 minutes, stirring or shaking often, until desired doneness.

Chocolate Marshmallows

Can of sweetened condensed milk	11 oz.	300 mL
Jar of marshmallow creme	7 oz.	198 g
Semi-sweet chocolate chips	2 1/3 cups	575 mL
Large marshmallows	60	60
Finely chopped walnuts (or pecans), toasted (see Note)	4 1/2 cups	1.1 L

Heat and stir condensed milk, marshmallow creme and chips in medium saucepan on low until smooth. Remove from heat.

Roll 1 marshmallow in chocolate mixture until coated using fork, allowing excess chocolate to drip back into saucepan. Roll in chopped walnuts in small bowl until coated. Place on waxed paper-lined baking sheet. Repeat with remaining marshmallows, chocolate mixture and walnuts. If chocolate mixture becomes too thick for dipping, reheat on low until desired consistency. Let marshmallows stand overnight until set. Makes 60 chocolate marshmallows.

1 chocolate marshmallow: 147 Calories; 8.3 g Total Fat (2.1 g Mono, 3.8 g Poly, 1.9 g Sat); 2 mg Cholesterol; 18 g Carbohydrate; 1 g Fibre; 3 g Protein; 14 mg Sodium

Pictured on page 101.

Cranberry Almond Bark

White chocolate bars (3 1/2 oz., 100 g, each), chopped	5	5
Whole almonds (with skin)	1 1/2 cups	375 mL
Dried cranberries	1 cup	250 mL

Homemade chocolate bark may not be much less expensive than store-bought, but it tastes so much better!

Heat chocolate in heavy medium saucepan on lowest heat, stirring often, until chocolate is almost melted. Do not overheat. Remove from heat. Stir until smooth.

Add almonds and cranberries. Stir until well coated. Spread on waxed paper-lined baking sheet with sides to 1/4 inch (6 mm) thickness. Chill until set. Break into irregular-shaped pieces, about 1 1/2 x 2 inches (3.8 x 5 cm) each. Makes about 56 pieces.

1 piece: 75 Calories; 4.8 g Total Fat (2.2 g Mono, 0.5 g Poly, 1.8 g Sat); 2 mg Cholesterol; 7 g Carbohydrate; 1 g Fibre; 1 g Protein; 8 mg Sodium

Pictured below.

Whether they've been naughty or nice, your guests deserve these melt-in-your-mouth truffles.

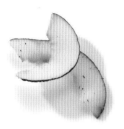

Apricot Brandy Truffles

Whipping cream	1/4 cup	60 mL
Butter (not margarine)	2 tbsp.	30 mL
White chocolate bars (3 1/2 oz., 100 g, each), finely chopped	3	3
Finely chopped dried apricots	3/4 cup	175 mL
Brandy (or 1 tsp., 5 mL, brandy flavouring)	1 tbsp.	15 mL
White chocolate melting wafers	1 cup	250 mL
Medium unsweetened coconut	1/4 cup	60 mL
Dark chocolate melting wafers	1 cup	250 mL

Heat and stir whipping cream and butter in small heavy saucepan on medium-high until boiling. Immediately remove from heat. Add chocolate bar pieces. Stir until chocolate is melted. Transfer to medium bowl.

Add apricot and brandy. Stir well. Chill, uncovered, for about 50 minutes, stirring twice, until just firm but not set. Roll into 25 balls, using 1 tbsp. (15 mL) for each. Chill for 30 minutes.

Heat white chocolate wafers in small heavy saucepan on lowest heat, stirring often, until almost melted. Do not overheat. Remove from heat. Stir until smooth. Dip 12 balls into white chocolate using fork, allowing excess to drip back into saucepan. Roll in coconut in small bowl. Place on waxed paper-lined baking sheet. If chocolate becomes too thick for dipping, reheat on low until desired consistency.

Heat dark chocolate wafers in separate small heavy saucepan on lowest heat, stirring often, until almost melted. Do not overheat. Remove from heat. Stir until smooth. Dip remaining balls into dark chocolate using fork, allowing excess to drip back into saucepan. Place on same baking sheet. If chocolate becomes too thick for dipping, reheat on low until desired consistency. Chill for about 30 minutes until set. Makes 25 truffles.

1 truffle: 168 Calories; 10.3 g Total Fat (3.1 g Mono, 0.3 g Poly, 6.3 g Sat); 10 mg Cholesterol; 19 g Carbohydrate; 1 g Fibre; 2 g Protein; 29 mg Sodium

Pictured on page 105.

Top: Rum Balls, page 106
Bottom: Apricot Brandy Truffles, above

A classic sweet for Christmas gift-giving.

Rum Balls

Chocolate cake mix (1 layer size)	1	1
Brown sugar, packed	1/4 cup	60 mL
Cocoa, sifted if lumpy	2 tbsp.	30 mL
Apricot jam	1/4 cup	60 mL
Dark (navy) rum	2 tbsp.	30 mL
Boiling water	1 tbsp.	15 mL
Chocolate sprinkles	1/2 – 3/4 cup	125 – 175 mL

Prepare and bake cake mix according to package directions. Let stand in pan on wire rack until cooled completely. Partially freeze. Crumble into large bowl.

Add brown sugar and cocoa. Stir.

Combine jam, rum and boiling water in small cup. Add to cake crumbs. Stir well. Shape into balls, using 1 1/2 tbsp. (25 mL) crumb mixture for each.

Roll each ball in chocolate sprinkles in small bowl. Chill. Makes 24 rum balls.

1 rum ball: 74 Calories; 1.8 g Total Fat (0.8 g Mono, 0.1 g Poly, 0.9 g Sat); 1 mg Cholesterol; 14 g Carbohydrate; trace Fibre; 1 g Protein; 89 mg Sodium

Pictured on page 105.

So pretty and such a sweet treat!

Pinwheels

Icing (confectioner's) sugar	2 1/2 cups	625 mL
Mashed potatoes	1/3 cup	75 mL
Vanilla	1/2 tsp.	2 mL
Salt	1/8 tsp.	0.5 mL
Icing (confectioner's) sugar, for dusting		
Smooth peanut butter	1/3 cup	75 mL

Combine first 4 ingredients in large bowl.

(continued on next page)

Turn out onto work surface dusted with icing sugar. Knead until smooth, adding more icing sugar if necessary, until a pliable but not sticky dough forms. Divide into 3 equal portions. Roll out 1 portion on surface dusted with icing sugar to 5 × 8 inch (12.5 × 20 cm) rectangle, 1/8 inch (3 mm) thick.

Spread about 1 1/2 tbsp. (25 mL) peanut butter evenly over top. Roll up, jelly roll-style, from long side. Wrap with plastic wrap. Chill. Repeat with remaining portions. Cut each roll into 1/4 inch (6 mm) slices. Makes about 6 dozen (72) pinwheels.

1 pinwheel: 25 Calories; 0.7 g Total Fat (0.3 g Mono, 0.2 g Poly, 0.1 g Sat); 0 mg Cholesterol; 5 g Carbohydrate; trace Fibre; 0 g Protein; 13 mg Sodium

Pictured below.

This is a soft, creamy fudge, so place in a sturdy container for gift-giving. A perfect blend of chocolate and peanuts.

note

To toast nuts, place in single layer in ungreased shallow pan. Bake in 350°F (175°C) oven for 5 to 8 minutes, stirring or shaking often, until desired doneness.

Choco-Peanut Fudge

Granulated sugar	2 cups	500 mL
Cocoa, sifted if lumpy	1/3 cup	75 mL
Milk	3/4 cup	175 mL
Golden corn syrup	2 tbsp.	30 mL
Hard margarine (or butter)	2 tbsp.	30 mL
Salt	1/8 tsp.	0.5 mL
Smooth peanut butter	1/3 cup	75 mL
Chopped unsalted peanuts (or walnuts), toasted (see Note)	1/2 cup	125 mL

Combine first 6 ingredients in large heavy saucepan. Bring to a boil on medium, stirring constantly. Reduce heat to medium-low. Brush side of saucepan with damp pastry brush to dissolve any sugar crystals. Simmer, uncovered, for about 30 minutes, without stirring, until mixture reaches soft ball stage: 234 to 240°F (112 to 116°C) on candy thermometer or until about 1/4 tsp. (1 mL) of mixture dropped into very cold water forms a soft ball that flattens on its own when removed. Let stand, without stirring, until bottom of saucepan is cool enough to touch.

Add peanut butter and peanuts. Beat with spoon until mixture loses its shine and pulls away from side of saucepan. Spread evenly in greased 8 × 8 inch (20 × 20 cm) pan. Chill until firm. Makes 1 1/2 lbs. (680 g) fudge. Cuts into 36 pieces.

1 piece: 86 Calories; 3.2 g Total Fat (1.6 g Mono, 0.8 g Poly, 0.6 g Sat); 0 mg Cholesterol; 14 g Carbohydrate; 1 g Fibre; 1 g Protein; 32 mg Sodium

Pictured on page 109.

Marshmallow creme adds a definite creaminess to this rich, sweet fudge.

White Creme Fudge

Granulated sugar	2 cups	500 mL
Half-and-half cream	2/3 cup	150 mL
Hard margarine (or butter)	1/4 cup	60 mL
White corn syrup	1 tbsp.	15 mL
White chocolate baking squares (1 oz., 28 g, each), chopped	8	8
Jar of marshmallow creme	7 oz.	198 g

(continued on next page)

Quartered glazed cherries	1/4 cup	60 mL

Heat and stir first 4 ingredients in large heavy saucepan on medium-low until boiling. Brush side of saucepan with damp pastry brush to dissolve any sugar crystals. Boil for about 30 minutes, without stirring, until mixture reaches soft ball stage: 234 to 240°F (112 to 116°C) on candy thermometer or until about 1/4 tsp. (1 mL) of mixture dropped into very cold water forms a soft ball that flattens on its own when removed. Remove from heat.

Add chocolate and marshmallow creme. Stir until chocolate is melted and mixture is smooth.

Add cherries. Stir. Spread evenly in greased 8 × 8 inch (20 × 20 cm) pan. Chill until firm. Makes about 2 lbs. (900 g) fudge. Cuts into 36 pieces.

1 piece: 120 Calories; 3.7 g Total Fat (1.6 g Mono, 0.2 g Poly, 1.7 g Sat); 3 mg Cholesterol; 22 g Carbohydrate; trace Fibre; 1 g Protein; 26 mg Sodium

Pictured below.

Inner Circle: White Creme Fudge, page 108
Outer Circle: Choco-Peanut Fudge, page 108

The ultimate snack for those who love white chocolate and caramel corn. The perfect pick-me-up.

note

To toast nuts, place in single layer in ungreased shallow pan. Bake in 350°F (175°C) oven for 5 to 8 minutes, stirring or shaking often, until desired doneness.

White Chocolate Popcorn

White chocolate bars (3 1/2 oz., 100 g, each), chopped	3	3
Bag of caramel-coated popcorn and peanuts (about 5 cups, 1.25 L)	7 oz.	200 g
Slivered almonds, toasted (see Note)	1/2 cup	125 mL

Heat chocolate in heavy medium saucepan on lowest heat, stirring often, until chocolate is almost melted. Do not overheat. Remove from heat. Stir until smooth.

Spread popcorn on foil-lined baking sheet with sides. Drizzle chocolate over popcorn. Stir. Sprinkle with almonds. Chill until set. Break into bite-size pieces. Makes about 5 1/2 cups (1.4 L).

1/2 cup (125 mL): 255 Calories; 13 g Total Fat (5.2 g Mono, 1.5 g Poly, 5.3 g Sat); 6 mg Cholesterol; 33 g Carbohydrate; 1 g Fibre; 4 g Protein; 79 mg Sodium

Pictured on page 111.

These take extra time, but are fun to make. Freeze in an airtight container.

Marshmallow Delights

Butterscotch toffee bars (such as Mackintosh's), 2 oz. (56 g) each, broken up	3	3
Sweetened condensed milk	2/3 cup	150 mL
Hard margarine (or butter)	1/4 cup	60 mL
Large marshmallows	30	30
Special K cereal	4 cups	1 L

Heat and stir toffee, condensed milk and margarine in small heavy saucepan on medium until toffee is melted and mixture is smooth. Remove from heat.

Dip 1 marshmallow in toffee mixture until coated using fork. If toffee mixture becomes too thick for dipping, reheat on medium until desired consistency.

(continued on next page)

Roll coated marshmallow in cereal in medium bowl until coated using fork. Place on waxed paper-lined baking sheet. Repeat with remaining marshmallows, toffee mixture and cereal. Let marshmallows stand until set. Makes 30.

1 marshmallow delight: 95 Calories; 2.5 g Total Fat (1.3 g Mono, 0.2 g Poly, 0.8 g Sat); 3 mg Cholesterol; 18 g Carbohydrate; trace Fibre; 1 g Protein; 63 mg Sodium

Pictured below.

Top Left: Marshmallow Delights, page 110
Top Right: White Chocolate Popcorn, page 110
Bottom: Crispy Roll, page 112

Crisp cereal roll with a yummy chocolate filling.

Crispy Roll

White corn syrup	1 cup	250 mL
Smooth peanut butter	1 cup	250 mL
Granulated sugar	1 cup	250 mL
Hard margarine (or butter)	3 tbsp.	50 mL
Crisp rice cereal	6 cups	1.5 L

FILLING

Icing (confectioner's) sugar	2 cups	500 mL
Cocoa, sifted if lumpy	1 cup	250 mL
Hard margarine (or butter), softened	1/2 cup	125 mL
Water	1/4 cup	60 mL
Vanilla	1 tsp.	5 mL

Heat and stir first 4 ingredients in large heavy saucepan on medium-high until boiling. Immediately remove from heat.

Add cereal. Stir until coated. Place sheet of waxed paper on damp work surface so paper will stay in place. Turn out cereal mixture onto waxed paper. Press into 10 x 15 inch (25 x 38 cm) rectangle. Let stand for 15 to 20 minutes until set, but still warm.

Filling: Beat all 5 ingredients on low in large bowl until combined. Beat on medium until smooth, adding more water if necessary until spreading consistency. Spread evenly over cereal mixture. Roll up, jelly roll-style, from long side, using waxed paper as guide. Wrap in plastic wrap. Chill. Cuts into 24 slices.

1 slice: 273 Calories; 11.8 g Total Fat (6.5 g Mono, 2.1 g Poly, 2.6 g Sat); 0 mg Cholesterol; 41 g Carbohydrate; 2 g Fibre; 4 g Protein; 202 mg Sodium

Pictured on page 111.

Frozen Cheesecake Bites

A creamy lemon cheesecake on a buttery shortbread base. Almonds add a crunch.

BOTTOM LAYER

All-purpose flour	1 1/2 cups	375 mL
Icing (confectioner's) sugar	2 tbsp.	30 mL
Sliced almonds	3/4 cup	175 mL
Hard margarine (or butter), softened, cut up	1/2 cup	125 mL

TOP LAYER

Blocks of cream cheese (8 oz., 250 g, each), softened	2	2
Container of lemon yogurt	6 oz.	175 mL
Large eggs	2	2
Granulated sugar	1/2 cup	125 mL
Cream of wheat (unprepared)	2 tbsp.	30 mL
Finely grated lemon zest	1 tbsp.	15 mL
Vanilla	1/2 tsp.	2 mL
Sliced almonds (optional)	1/4 cup	60 mL

Bottom Layer: Combine first 3 ingredients in medium bowl. Cut in margarine until mixture resembles coarse crumbs. Press firmly in greased 9 × 13 inch (22 × 33 cm) pan. Bake in 350°F (175°C) oven for 10 minutes. Let stand in pan on wire rack for 5 minutes.

Top Layer: Beat first 7 ingredients in medium bowl until smooth. Spread evenly over bottom layer.

Sprinkle second amount of almonds over top. Bake for 25 to 30 minutes until set and edges are golden. Let stand in pan on wire rack until cooled completely. Cut into 15 rectangles with a wet knife. Cut each rectangle diagonally to make 2 triangles, for a total of 30 triangles. Arrange triangles 1/2 inch (12 mm) apart on ungreased baking sheet. Freeze for 2 to 3 hours until firm. Store in resealable freezer bags or tins, separating layers with waxed paper. Freeze until ready to serve. Makes 30.

1 cheesecake bite: 157 Calories; 11 g Total Fat (4.9 g Mono, 0.9 g Poly, 4.6 g Sat); 33 mg Cholesterol; 12 g Carbohydrate; 1 g Fibre; 3 g Protein; 95 mg Sodium

Pictured on page 115.

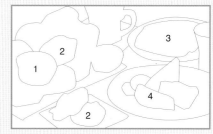

Photo Legend next page
1. Chipper Muffins, page 116
2. Butterscotch Muffins, page 116
3. Lemon Loaf, page 117
4. Frozen Cheesecake Bites, this page

Imagine the cheers you'll receive when you bring these golden treats to the office for coffee break.

Butterscotch Muffins

Hard margarine (or butter), softened	6 tbsp.	100 mL
Brown sugar, packed	1/4 cup	60 mL
Large egg	1	1
Milk	1 1/4 cups	300 mL
All-purpose flour	2 cups	500 mL
Box of instant butterscotch pudding powder (4 serving size)	4 oz.	113 g
Butterscotch chips	2/3 cup	150 mL
Baking powder	1 tbsp.	15 mL
Salt	1/2 tsp.	2 mL

Beat margarine and brown sugar in large bowl until light and creamy. Add egg. Beat. Add milk. Beat well.

Combine remaining 5 ingredients in medium bowl. Make a well in centre. Add margarine mixture to well. Stir until just moistened. Grease 12 muffin cups with cooking spray. Fill cups 3/4 full. Bake in 400°F (205°C) oven for about 18 minutes until golden, and wooden pick inserted in centre of muffin comes out clean. Let stand in pan for 5 minutes before removing to wire rack to cool. Makes 12 muffins.

1 muffin: 231 Calories; 7.2 g Total Fat (4.1 g Mono, 0.8 g Poly, 1.7 g Sat); 20 mg Cholesterol; 39 g Carbohydrate; 1 g Fibre; 4 g Protein; 405 mg Sodium

Pictured on page 114.

A double chocolate treat. Great snacking.

Chipper Muffins

All-purpose flour	1 3/4 cups	425 mL
Semi-sweet chocolate chips	1 cup	250 mL
Granulated sugar	3/4 cup	175 mL
Cocoa, sifted if lumpy	1/3 cup	75 mL
Baking powder	1 tbsp.	15 mL
Salt	1/2 tsp.	2 mL
Large egg	1	1
Milk	1 cup	250 mL
Cooking oil	1/3 cup	75 mL
Vanilla	1 tsp.	5 mL

(continued on next page)

Combine first 6 ingredients in medium bowl. Make a well in centre.

Beat egg in small bowl. Add milk, cooking oil and vanilla. Stir. Pour into well. Stir until just moistened. Grease 12 muffin cups with cooking spray. Fill cups 3/4 full. Bake in 400ºF (205ºC) oven for about 20 minutes until golden, and wooden pick inserted in centre of muffin comes out clean. Let stand in pan for 5 minutes before removing to wire rack to cool. Makes 12 muffins.

1 muffin: 271 Calories; 12 g Total Fat (5.6 g Mono, 2.2 g Poly, 3.6 g Sat); 19 mg Cholesterol; 40 g Carbohydrate; 2 g Fibre; 4 g Protein; 210 mg Sodium

Pictured on page 114.

Lemon Loaf

Hard margarine (or butter), softened	1/2 cup	125 mL
Granulated sugar	1 cup	250 mL
Large eggs	2	2
Milk	1/2 cup	125 mL
All-purpose flour	1 1/2 cups	375 mL
Grated lemon peel	1 tbsp.	15 mL
Baking powder	1 tsp.	5 mL
Salt	1/2 tsp.	2 mL
LEMON GLAZE		
Lemon juice	1/3 cup	75 mL
Granulated sugar	1/4 cup	60 mL

The glaze completes the delightful flavour of this loaf.

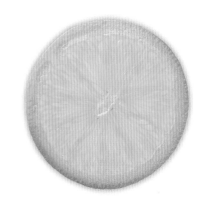

Cream margarine and sugar in large bowl. Add eggs, 1 at a time, beating well after each addition. Add milk. Beat well.

Combine next 4 ingredients in small bowl. Add to margarine mixture. Stir until just moistened. Spread evenly in greased 9 x 5 x 3 inch (22 x 12.5 x 7.5 cm) loaf pan. Bake in 350ºF (175ºC) oven for about 60 minutes until wooden pick inserted in centre comes out clean.

Lemon Glaze: Heat and stir lemon juice and sugar in small saucepan on medium until sugar is dissolved. Spoon evenly over top of hot loaf. Let stand for 10 minutes before removing from pan to wire rack to cool. Cuts into 16 slices.

1 slice: 177 Calories; 6.9 g Total Fat (4.2 g Mono, 0.7 g Poly, 1.5 g Sat); 27 mg Cholesterol; 27 g Carbohydrate; trace Fibre; 2 g Protein; 180 mg Sodium

Pictured on page 115.

A tender loaf with a delicate apple flavour.

note

To toast nuts, place in single layer in ungreased shallow pan. Bake in 350°F (175°C) oven for 5 to 8 minutes, stirring or shaking often, until desired doneness.

Apple Loaf

Hard margarine (or butter), softened	1/2 cup	125 mL
Granulated sugar	1 cup	250 mL
Large eggs	2	2
Milk	1/3 cup	75 mL
Vanilla	1 tsp.	5 mL
Coarsely grated, tart cooking apple (such as Granny Smith), with peel, packed	1 cup	250 mL
All-purpose flour	2 cups	500 mL
Baking powder	1 tsp.	5 mL
Baking soda	1/2 tsp.	2 mL
Salt	1/2 tsp.	2 mL
Chopped walnuts, toasted (see Note)	1/2 cup	125 mL

Cream margarine and sugar in large bowl. Add eggs, 1 at a time, beating well after each addition. Add milk and vanilla. Beat.

Add apple. Stir.

Combine remaining 5 ingredients in medium bowl. Add to apple mixture. Stir until just moistened. Spread evenly in greased 9 x 5 x 3 inch (22 x 12.5 x 7.5 cm) loaf pan. Bake in 350°F (175°C) oven for about 60 minutes until wooden pick inserted in centre comes out clean. Let stand in pan for 10 minutes before removing to wire rack to cool. Cuts into 16 slices.

1 slice: 207 Calories; 9.2 g Total Fat (4.7 g Mono, 2.3 g Poly, 1.7 g Sat); 27 mg Cholesterol; 28 g Carbohydrate; 1 g Fibre; 4 g Protein; 219 mg Sodium

Pictured on page 119.

Comfort is sitting down and enjoying this muffin with a cup of your favourite hot beverage. Great served any time.

Apple Streusel Muffins

TOPPING

Brown sugar, packed	1/2 cup	125 mL
All-purpose flour	1/4 cup	60 mL
Ground cinnamon	1/4 tsp.	1 mL
Hard margarine (or butter), softened	1/4 cup	60 mL
All-purpose flour	1 1/2 cups	375 mL
Granulated sugar	1/2 cup	125 mL
Baking powder	1 tbsp.	15 mL
Salt	1/2 tsp.	2 mL
Large egg	1	1
Milk	2/3 cup	150 mL
Cooking oil	1/4 cup	60 mL
Peeled, shredded cooking apple (such as McIntosh), packed	3/4 cup	175 mL

Topping: Combine brown sugar, flour and cinnamon in small bowl. Cut in margarine until mixture resembles coarse crumbs. Set aside.

Combine next 4 ingredients in large bowl. Make a well in centre.

Beat egg, milk and cooking oil in small bowl. Add apple. Stir. Pour into well. Stir until just moistened. Grease 12 muffin cups with cooking spray. Fill cups 3/4 full. Divide and sprinkle topping over each. Bake in 400°F (205°C) oven for 15 to 20 minutes until golden, and wooden pick inserted in centre of muffin comes out clean. Let stand in pan for 5 minutes before removing to wire rack to cool. Makes 12 muffins.

1 muffin: 237 Calories; 9.7 g Total Fat (5.7 g Mono, 2 g Poly, 1.4 g Sat); 19 mg Cholesterol; 35 g Carbohydrate; 1 g Fibre; 3 g Protein; 256 mg Sodium

Pictured on page 121.

*Small melt-in-your-mouth mints.
Cutting them with scissors gives them
a pretty look.*

After-Dinner Mints

Envelopes of unflavoured gelatin (1 tbsp., 15 mL, each)	3	3
Cold water	1/2 cup	125 mL
Icing (confectioner's) sugar	2 cups	500 mL
Peppermint flavouring	1 1/2 tsp.	7 mL
Baking powder	1/4 tsp.	1 mL
Icing (confectioner's) sugar	4 cups	1 L

Sprinkle gelatin over water in medium saucepan. Let stand for 1 minute. Heat and stir on low until gelatin is dissolved. Remove from heat.

Add first amount of icing sugar, peppermint flavouring and baking powder. Stir well.

Add second amount of icing sugar. Stir. Mixture will be sticky. Turn out onto work surface dusted with icing sugar. Knead dough for about 1 minute until smooth. Divide into 4 equal portions. Cover 3 portions with plastic wrap to prevent drying. Roll out 1 portion into 1/2 inch (12 mm) diameter rope. Slice into 1/2 inch (12 mm) pieces with scissors or knife. Arrange in single layer on waxed paper-lined baking sheet. Repeat with remaining portions. Let stand for about 1 hour until firm. Store in resealable plastic bags. Makes about 168 mints.

1 mint: 18 Calories; 0 g Total Fat (0 g Mono, 0 g Poly, 0 g Sat); 0 mg Cholesterol; 5 g Carbohydrate; 0 g Fibre; 0 g Protein; 1 mg Sodium

Pictured on page 123.

*An all-chocolate, creamy, don't-have-
to-wait-until-after-eight mint.*

note

A few more drops of flavouring may be added to dough to increase mint flavour.

Fudgy Chocolate Mints

Semi-sweet chocolate chips	2 cups	500 mL
Can of sweetened condensed milk	11 oz.	300 mL
Milk chocolate chips	1 cup	250 mL
Hard margarine (or butter)	2 tbsp.	30 mL
Vanilla	1 tsp.	5 mL
Peppermint flavouring (see Note)	1/8 tsp.	0.5 mL

(continued on next page)

Heat and stir all 6 ingredients in large heavy saucepan on medium-low until chocolate is melted and mixture is smooth. Spread evenly in greased or foil-lined 9 × 9 inch (22 × 22 cm) pan. Let stand until set. Cut into 12 rows lengthwise and crosswise, for a total of 144 mints.

1 mint: 28 Calories; 1.5 g Total Fat (0.5 g Mono, 0.1 g Poly, 0.9 g Sat); 1 mg Cholesterol; 4 g Carbohydrate; trace Fibre; 0 g Protein; 7 mg Sodium

Pictured below.

variation

For small candies, drop, using 2 tsp. (10 mL) for each, onto waxed paper. Let stand until set. If chocolate mixture becomes too hard to drop, reheat on low until desired consistency.

Left: Fudgy Chocolate Mints, page 122
Right: After-Dinner Mints, page 122

Throughout this book measurements are given in Conventional and Metric measure. To compensate for differences between the two measurements due to rounding, a full metric measure is not always used. The cup used is the standard 8 fluid ounce. Temperature is given in degrees Fahrenheit and Celsius. Baking pan measurements are in inches and centimetres as well as quarts and litres. An exact metric conversion is given on this page as well as the working equivalent (Metric Standard Measure).

Pans

Conventional – Inches	Metric – Centimetres
8 × 8 inch	20 × 20 cm
9 × 9 inch	22 × 22 cm
9 × 13 inch	22 × 33 cm
10 × 15 inch	25 × 38 cm
11 × 17 inch	28 × 43 cm
8 × 2 inch round	20 × 5 cm
9 × 2 inch round	22 × 5 cm
10 × 4 1/2 inch tube	25 × 11 cm
8 × 4 × 3 inch loaf	20 × 10 × 7.5 cm
9 × 5 × 3 inch loaf	22 × 12.5 × 7.5 cm

Oven Temperatures

Fahrenheit (°F)	Celsius (°C)	Fahrenheit (°F)	Celsius (°C)
175°	80°	350°	175°
200°	95°	375°	190°
225°	110°	400°	205°
250°	120°	425°	220°
275°	140°	450°	230°
300°	150°	475°	240°
325°	160°	500°	260°

Spoons

Conventional Measure	Metric Exact Conversion Millilitre (mL)	Metric Standard Measure Millilitre (mL)
1/8 teaspoon (tsp.)	0.6 mL	0.5 mL
1/4 teaspoon (tsp.)	1.2 mL	1 mL
1/2 teaspoon (tsp.)	2.4 mL	2 mL
1 teaspoon (tsp.)	4.7 mL	5 mL
2 teaspoons (tsp.)	9.4 mL	10 mL
1 tablespoon (tbsp.)	14.2 mL	15 mL

Cups

1/4 cup (4 tbsp.)	56.8 mL	60 mL
1/3 cup (5 1/3 tbsp.)	75.6 mL	75 mL
1/2 cup (8 tbsp.)	113.7 mL	125 mL
2/3 cup (10 2/3 tbsp.)	151.2 mL	150 mL
3/4 cup (12 tbsp.)	170.5 mL	175 mL
1 cup (16 tbsp.)	227.3 mL	250 mL
4 1/2 cups	1022.9 mL	1000 mL(1 L)

Dry Measurements

Conventional Measure Ounces (oz.)	Metric Exact Conversion Grams (g)	Metric Standard Measure Grams (g)
1 oz.	28.3 g	28 g
2 oz.	56.7 g	57 g
3 oz.	85.0 g	85 g
4 oz.	113.4 g	125 g
5 oz.	141.7 g	140 g
6 oz.	170.1 g	170 g
7 oz.	198.4 g	200 g
8 oz.	226.8 g	250 g
16 oz.	453.6 g	500 g
32 oz.	907.2 g	1000 g (1 kg)

Casseroles

Canada & Britain		United States	
Standard Size Casserole	Exact Metric Measure	Standard Size Casserole	Exact Metric Measure
1 qt. (5 cups)	1.13 L	1 qt. (4 cups)	900 mL
1 1/2 qts. (7 1/2 cups)	1.69 L	1 1/2 qts. (6 cups)	1.35 L
2 qts. (10 cups)	2.25 L	2 qts. (8 cups)	1.8 L
2 1/2 qts. (12 1/2 cups)	2.81 L	2 1/2 qts. (10 cups)	2.25 L
3 qts. (15 cups)	3.38 L	3 qts. (12 cups)	2.7 L
4 qts. (20 cups)	4.5 L	4 qts. (16 cups)	3.6 L
5 qts. (25 cups)	5.63 L	5 qts. (20 cups)	4.5 L